GROW 10X WITH CRO

"The Step-by-Step System For Boosting Your Online Conversions"

ANTHONY LA ROCCA

Table of Contents

Grow 10X with CRO

The Ultimate Guide To Maximizing Your Online Conversions

This publication is designed to provide accurate and authoritative information regarding the subject matter covered. It is sold with the understanding that the publisher is not engaged in rendering legal, accounting, or other professional services. If you require legal advice or other expert assistance, you should seek the services of a competent professional.

Disclaimer: The author makes no guarantees to the results you'll achieve by reading this book. All business requires risk and hard work. Your results may vary when undertaking any new business venture or marketing strategy.

"You will get all you want in life if you help enough other people get what they want."
- Zig Ziglar

How I've Made A Fortune With CRO (And You Can Too)

Hi, I'm Anthony La Rocca. I began my Internet Marketing journey when I was only twelve years old. The year was 1999, and the business world was just beginning to realize the incredible possibilities of this new technology. Since then, I've generated more than $100M+ in sales for my clients.

It has been an incredible journey.

I'm thankful to my parents, brother, pets, and all other family and friends who have helped shape me into the person I am today.

And of course, I'm just as grateful to the countless clients who I've been lucky enough to work with. I've learned so much from all of them, and it has been so rewarding to watch their profits take off.

After many years of being a consultant for dozens of brands around the world, I went on to launch my own conversion growth agency, CRO Profits, which is regularly helping clients multiply their conversions by **10X**.

With all of this valuable experience that has been gained, I decided these "secrets" that I had discovered were too good to keep to myself.

I believe that you too, can multiply your conversions **10X**.

And in this book, I will show you exactly how to do it.

And I've done this for 2 simple reasons:

> **Reason #1:** There is a better way to increase conversions for any business.
> **Reason #2:** To quickly help you make **more money** following Reason #1

Conversion Rate Optimization, or "CRO" as we will refer to it from here on out, is the secret to any online sales operation. It is what separates success from failure.

I won't lie and tell you that it is simple, but I assure you, if you're reading this book, a firm understanding of CRO is well within your grasp.

Because of my mastery of CRO, I have become a 'go- to guy' for some of the biggest eCommerce operations in the world. I've helped countless companies multiply their sales tenfold, and even became a bestselling author. I'm constantly in demand as a consultant and my coaching programs sell out almost instantly.

I've worked relentlessly to keep up with the seemingly endless wave of Internet Marketing evolutions. I wasn't sure exactly where the industry was going, but there is one thing I was certain of still to this day:

*There is **a lot of money** for **you** to make online. The key is mastering the profitable world of conversions.*

I'm not telling you this to be boastful. In fact, it's just the opposite. And am not some kind of Harvard- educated marketing genius.

I'm just a guy who spent twenty years learning every little detail about online sales I could find.

I traveled the world to study with some of the most famous minds in the business world.

I experimented, tested, failed, succeeded, then failed again.

Much of my consistent success can be attributed to a commitment to constant learning. I have been refining my techniques non- stop, learning new things with every project I take on. I hope you will embrace that spirit as well!

There is always something new to learn, and every successful entrepreneur I know would agree with that statement.

After endless hours of refinement, I finally began to discover the strategies that inevitably lead to massive growth in sales. And they are all compiled right here, in this book.

If you implement everything done for you in this book, it will be almost impossible for your sales not to grow.

I truly believe that whether you are running a global eCommerce brand or just a small local online business, if you make every effort to learn and take action with all systems taught in this book, you will be set up to quickly grow your conversions and sales!

Again, I don't say this to be boastful. I say it because I've seen it work. Time and time again.

The materials in this book are the result of a long career spent studying the great salesmen that came before me.

I was lucky enough to study in person multiple times with the legendary sales king, Dan Kennedy. My other notable sales mentors include globally renowned Bob Proctor, Seth Godin, Frank Kern, Chris Record, Neil Patel, Sean Mize, Mark Cuban, Russel Brunson, Grant Cardone, and most recently, Gary Vaynerchuk.

So remember, you don't have to take my word for it.

The conversion techniques you are about to learn have been building fortunes for generations.

Your successful competitors are already doing this. So don't wait any longer.

I knew from the start that these techniques would be helpful to just about anyone. It would be a mistake to think that they only work for "traditional" businesses. These strategies can help an abstract painter get more commissions or a dog walker to get more clients.

Is every technique going to work perfectly for everyone? Of course not. Approach this book with an open mind, and a willingness to experiment. Eventually, you will develop your own foolproof CRO methods that will lead you to lots of conversions and sales too.

If you decide help is needed implementing these conversions boosting strategies quickly, please book a call to chat with me and my team by going here:
CROProfits.com/call

Helping people like you to **10x** conversions is exactly what we do day-in and day-out.

In the following pages, you will receive a detailed conversion guide that will painlessly take you from novice to expert. And best of all, it won't take you twenty years of study.

Instead, by adhering to the plan, focusing on small victories, and staying dedicated to your ultimate vision, you will inevitably see the results you want within as little as a few weeks.

Now, let's get you started!

Chapter One:

What Is CRO?

"Far and away the best prize that life offers is the chance to work hard at work worth doing."
– Theodore Roosevelt

In this chapter you will learn:

- ✓ What CRO Is
- ✓ How CRO Can Improve Your Bottom Line
- ✓ Why CRO Has Become Such a Hot Topic
- ✓ How To Calculate Your Current CR%
- ✓ What CRO Techniques You Should Avoid At All Costs
- ✓ How To Think Like a CRO PRO

Simply put, CRO is the art and science of turning visitors on your webpage into paying customers. It is the formula that allows you to:

- ✓ Increase sales
- ✓ Connect with your most profitable customers
- ✓ Lower acquisition costs

I'm consistently surprised at how many people overlook CRO. Considering the exponential benefits it brings to a business, you would think there would be a surplus of reliable information out there. And yet, there isn't. It's a source of frustration for countless people.

One common mistake is to get hyper fixated on increasing traffic. Sure, it would be great to double your traffic, but if no one is spending any money, what good does that do? It's like pouring water into a bucket with a hole in the bottom. It looks like you're making progress, but you never actually increase profit.

CRO lets us plug up those metaphorical holes in the bucket. It identifies the areas of your website that need improvement. Maybe it's a broken link, an off- putting headline, a product page that takes too long to load. Whatever it is, it's probably right under your nose. And you might not know what it is until you do some testing. (much more on that later)

The CRO Boom

It is only recently that CRO has emerged as one of the hottest topics in the business world. Like all great business innovations, this is the result of a lot of great minds working together and separately across a wide variety of industries, and coming together with a set of rules that seem to lead to an inevitable boost in conversions.

What I love most about the techniques that make up my CRO philosophy is how adaptable they are.

So many people are setting out on their own, turning their passions into businesses, and making those businesses their main source of income. Some people are thriving in well established industries like landscaping, fashion, or music. Others are building global communities around niche interests - selling to people that would have been completely unreachable a generation ago.

But no matter what your area of focus is, there remains one simple truth - you have to convert.

Calculating Your Conversion Rate

The first step in optimizing your conversion rate is knowing exactly what it is. The formula for calculating CR looks like this:

$$\frac{\text{Number Of Conversions}}{\text{Total Visitors}} \times 100$$

So for example, let's say 20,000 people visit your page. 500 of them make a purchase. This would make your conversion rate 2.5%.

It is estimated that most businesses have a CR of anywhere from 0.5% to 6%, with 6% being an extremely high performer.

Now, let's say you follow the methods set out in the following chapters. You improve upon your design, get rid of the dead weight that is slowing down your page (trust me it's there), and you fill your page with engaging, interactive content. Out of those 20,000 visitors, 1000 of them make a purchase. As a result, your conversion rate is now 5%, setting you on the path to becoming a top performer.

Consider how that kind of growth would affect your business:

Best of all, you've done this without spending more money on advertising, meaning that new revenue is pure profit.

Becoming a CRO Master

As I stated at the beginning of this chapter, CRO is a potent mix of art and science. When you combine technical know-how, with an awareness of buyer psychology, you'll be amazed at the growth you'll see.

In the following chapters, we will begin the nitty gritty technical work.

But before we move on, there are a few key tactics from across the business world that you need to understand.

- Understand Your Customer

Sales Master Dan Kennedy wrote that the first complete step to making a sale is to "analyze thoroughly, understand, and connect with the customer." All too often, marketers focus on what customers 'should' do and not what they 'actually' do. Focus on creating a user experience that the customer enjoys. Find ways to make them want to stay on your page, and willingly go further into your sales funnel.

- You Are Here To Improve Your Customer's Life

Whether you are selling a t-shirt that makes them look good, food they enjoy, or a program that will make their professional job easier, customers are solely focused on improving their lives.

If you can improve your customer's life, they will happily spend their money with you.

Keep this rule in the back of your mind at all times, especially when we begin editing your copy and web design.

- CRO% Is A Moving Target

Average CR %'s vary by location, industry, etc. There's no magic number to aim for. The true CRO masters are always looking for ways to improve. Even the slightest tweak can give you a major boost in revenue.

A Few Quick Notes On What Not To Do

You know those click-bait filled websites that bombard you with pop-up ads right away? Think of how you feel when you open one of those pages. Do you want to spend your time and money there? Of course not! You probably wouldn't trust them with your email address, never mind your credit card information.

We are going to spend a lot of time looking at positive examples that you should be following.
But I believe it is equally valuable to learn from bad examples. Not just the outrageously bad ones, but the average experiences that feel like they could be so much better.

Once you start studying CRO, your online shopping experience will never be the same. You'll start to notice every little detail of an online store. The same way an art student can see details in a painting that are invisible to the average person, you will start to understand the meaning behind the designs of the websites you visit.

PRO TIP: Keep a file on your computer where you can make notes. Try to write down one good thing you learned from a different website every day. That way, if you ever feel like you are stuck in a rut, you'll have a swipe file of resources that you can always turn to for inspiration.

Setting Achievable Goals

I personally recommend setting small goals, and doing everything in your power to achieve them. For example, let's say that your site is currently converting at .5%, and that is just not good enough. Our ultimate goal is to boost that rate **10X** right?

You can do it, but you can't do it all at once. Pick a reasonable goal, say doubling your conversions in the next month. Maybe you pick one specific technique and really focus on it. Then, before you know it, you're at 1%. It may not sound like much, but it is a terrific start.

Make sure you take the time to acknowledge and congratulate yourself for your small victories!

Success in conversions is like success in anything else. The first few steps are the hardest. From there, things can start to snowball and build momentum in ways you may have never thought possible.

That 1% conversion rate? Now you've proven that you have the capability to double it. So pick a new technique, and focus all your energy on that.

Maybe that new landing page is great, but you need to make some adjustments to your checkout page.

Maybe moving that 'Pay Now' button to the top right of the screen and simplifying the design is enough to boost you to 2%.

Keep testing, keep trying new things, and keep improving. Before you know it, that 10X growth will be a reality.

And therein lies the beauty of CRO. There are so many details, so many opportunities to make an average store good and a good store great. I've been doing this for years now and I am still never tired of the process. Approach this enthusiastically, and I sincerely believe you'll start to love it as much as I do!

Before you go any further, stop and ask yourself the following questions?

☐ Do I have a good understanding of the concept of Conversion Rate Optimization?

_____

☐ Am I prepared to work hard at every aspect of this complex topic?

_____

☐ What specific goals can I achieve through a better understanding of CRO?

_____

Chapter Two:
What CRO Mastery Can Do For You

> *"You only have to do a few things right in your life so long as you don't do too many things wrong."*
> *– Warren Buffett*

In this chapter you will learn:

- ✓ How An Ordinary Person Came To Master CRO

- ✓ The Tools and Mindset You Needed

I never had a traditional 'A-ha!' moment, where a lightbulb went off over my head and suddenly I had mastered CRO.

Instead, it was more like a hundred little moments.

They came to me through endless trial and error, minor discoveries, and occasional large leaps forward.

It was an exhausting process, but the rewards have been immense.

My big break, so to speak, came when I was hired by a now globally recognized D2C fashion company to find a solution for their ongoing sales slump.

At the time, they only had eight employees (now they have nearly three hundred, and offices around the world). The company was profitable, but just barely, and for months they had been struggling to build any momentum.

Being the ambitious young marketer I was, I felt confident that I could answer their problems. In doing so, I laid the groundwork for a CRO philosophy that now consistently generates major profits for countless companies.

But back then, I was starting from scratch. This was the early days of internet marketing, before tools like Shopify and Facebook made eCommerce accessible to the common person.

All I had was a set of analytics, some sales reports, and access to the company's day to day operations.

The first thing I realized is that no one was taking the time to study the little details of the web operation.

And it's hard to blame them!

Like most business people, they were immersed in their jobs while trying to manage their family lives and find time for the occasional good night's sleep.

How were they supposed to find time to split test long form and short form copy, analyze the details of their customers' online behavior, and test product page loading times?

Well, it turned out that these seemingly small details were anything but small.

Over the next year or so, I studied and tested just about every detail of that website.

I found that certain details really were inconsequential. Others made all the difference in the world.

I was able to do this because I brought an inquisitive mind and a new perspective to the job.

For many workers, every day feels like a broken record. You show up, do the same job you did yesterday, and go home without discovering anything new. Then tomorrow comes and you do the same thing all over. No wonder they were in a sales slump.

I suspect for many business owners, this is all too common.

You're working hard and you're frustrated at your lack of progress. You know there is a problem, but you don't know where to look.

But if you can alter your thinking patterns, you can start to see some of the weak spots that are preventing you from making the gains you deserve.

As I analyzed this company's webpage, I saw several obvious issues.

Some of the images were low quality, even a little blurry.

The page titles were too long.

The product descriptions were bland and technical.

When someone sees a low quality image, they subconsciously start to associate your product with low quality.

A long page title takes too long to read and doesn't immediately draw you in.

And for 99% of customers, technical jargon is straight up boring.

So we fixed all of that. Good start. But it wasn't enough.

Next, we installed heat mapping software on the website. This allowed us to track exactly how visitors to the page were behaving. Some were going to the homepage and then leaving immediately. Some spent a long time browsing product pages but ultimately never made a purchase. Once we understood their behavior, we were able to tweak the page to make their experience smoother and more enjoyable.

Then, we started analyzing prices. We tested different prices for the same project – $9.91, $9.95, $9.99, etc. You wouldn't think that an eight cent price change would make much of a difference, but it did! We realized that prices ending in '9' lead to significantly more conversions. Another tiny detail that leads to more conversions. Who knew?

From there, the possibilities were endless. We tested different color schemes, different fonts and text sizes, page formats, everything you can imagine.

And here is the best part: Once you've done the research, there's no more guesswork. You know exactly what works. You implement the necessary changes. You watch your sales numbers grow.

Eventually, that company multiplied its sales by ten. Can you imagine what your life would be like if you could multiply your income by ten?

Now, at a time when businesses are failing left and right, that company continues to post record profits. They've even established an entire department to continuously monitor the CRO techniques I implemented.

Getting In The Right Mindset

Sometimes, when I begin a CRO consultation with a new client, they get overwhelmed. They might even get discouraged when I point out all the areas they need to improve. Here is what I always tell them: You should be excited about this!

The reason you're not making sales has nothing to do with the quality of your products. On the contrary, your customers want to spend their money! They just need to be nudged in the right direction.

I often tell clients that positive in = positive out - meaning start your day telling yourself you will grow your conversions by 10x. Say this to yourself at least 3 times daily. Any free time, listening to motivational podcasts - or- marketing podcasts about increasing conversions. The more negativity you cut out in your life, the more space you leave to invite in positive results!

As you progress through this book, I urge you to never get discouraged. Every time you discover a "flaw" in your operation, view it as an opportunity to grow. The more opportunities you find during your self analysis, the larger your growth will be!

Hopefully, you are now inspired, energized, and ready to take the eCommerce world by storm. Before you go any further ask yourself this one question:

☐ *Am I ready to become a CRO Master?*

Chapter Three:

Make A Great First Impression With Your Homepage

> *"The first one gets the oyster, the second gets the shell."*
> *– Andrew Carnegie*

In this chapter you will learn:

- ✓ The True Purpose of a Homepage (It's not what most people think)

- ✓ How Your Homepage Can Make Or Break You

- ✓ The Most Common Homepage Mistake

- ✓ How To Get Visitors From Homepage to Checkout

A perfectly designed homepage is precisely what is needed to multiply your conversions. It establishes your brand, welcomes your customer, and offers them a glimpse of the great experience they are about to have. But there is one thing that this very important page is not meant to do...

Homepages Are Not For Selling

This is the most common mistake I see, and I see it over and over again. Whenever I see someone trying to make sales through their homepage, I see money flying out the window. It just doesn't work.

Your homepage is your opportunity to convey the most important aspects of your business to your client in as concise a manner as possible.

If your homepage is loaded with images, links, articles, and deals, people will get overloaded. It happens at a subconscious level. They see a huge amount of information that they are not ready for, and thus, they leave, most likely never to return.

Picture yourself walking into a shopping mall. Imagine that right after opening the door, you are mobbed by vendors from every store. They're waving coupons at you, shouting about the deals they offer, and saying "BUY BUY BUY!"

Most sane people would turn and run.

In the real world, you enter a shopping mall and are greeted by a pleasant map, showing you where everything is. Since you happen to be in the market for a new pair of jeans, you casually find all the clothing outlets that interest you and take a pleasant stroll to the store. When you arrive at your destination, you find exactly what you want, sitting on the shelves, waiting for you to happily make your purchase.

This is the perfect blueprint for your homepage.

The ideal homepage features:

- Pleasant colors and imagery

- A few of your top products

- A handful of glowing reviews/testimonials

- A subtle banner for a current special/sale

- A live chat pop-up

- Contact information

Anything more is too much!

You may be asking, "Ok, so if my homepage doesn't make sales, how do I get clients to go to the actual product pages?"

Simple.

First - Add a navigation header featuring your 3 to 5 most accessed pages.
Then - Add a footer with the same 3- 5 links. This footer can also include columns of text linking to your top 10- 20 pages (if applicable).

By doing this, you give your customer multiple opportunities to see what you're offering without overwhelming them. If your homepage is well designed, your customer will be eager to see more. Remember, they came to your page for a reason. Make their experience pleasant, and they will be happy to stick around.

Case Studies

I'd like to direct your attention to two brilliantly designed homepages.

One is for a majorly recognized construction chain with stores all over the world. The other is a niche boutique clothing store operating out of Brooklyn. They both dramatically outsell their competition.

Let's take a look at what makes these two very different brands so successful.

Home Depot

Home Depot's online sales operation brought in nearly $1.7 billion (1,700,000,000) dollars in 2021, making it the eighth most successful eCommerce operation in the world. Their closest competitor brought in less than half of that. Both websites have similar inventory.

So what makes Home Depot so successful? Let's dive in.

Go to your computer and type in HomeDepot.com. The first thing you see is a pleasant picture of a well decorated kitchen. It is accompanied by the words "Special Buy," and a link that says "Shop Now." Notice they're not trying to sell you anything right away? They show you what you came to see, and offer you the opportunity to shop for it if you choose.

That kitchen image is on a scroll bar. After a moment, it will be replaced by an image of a work area, complete with a wall full of hammers, saws, etc. This image is accompanied by the phrase "Up to 40% off." Notice that they show these two images separately to avoid information overload.

And yet, within five seconds of visiting the webpage, I've already gotten a glimpse of how nice my house could look and how much more work I could get done by shopping here. Excellently done.

Now, Let's take a look at the header. In small letters, it lists the most commonly visited pages: 'Home Decor, Furniture, and Kitchenware,' 'DIY Projects,' etc. These links don't jump right out at you, but they are there when you're ready for them. The pages and the products they represent are organized and categorized in an easy to understand way. Despite the thousands of products available, it's not difficult to find what you're looking for.

As we begin to scroll down the page, we see a few more products get introduced. This time, the images are small - about thumbnail size. This gives a nice contrast to the top of the page.

We see short phrases - "Free Delivery," "Brighten Your Room," and "Bath Savings." - They are easy to read and reinforce the customer's interest.

Now scroll all the way to the bottom. We see a horizontal bar featuring their slogan "How doers get more done." Again, brand reinforcement meant to lodge Home Depot into your memory. And at the very bottom of the page, we again see 'Popular Categories' and columns with links to 'Customer Service,' 'Resources,' 'About Us,' etc.

To summarize, Home Depot's homepage has

- Eye catching imagery

- Brand consistency
- Enticing Offers

- Easily Navigable menus.

And as a result, HomeDepot.com is one of the most profitable websites in the world.

Quaker Marine

Now let's take a look at a very different, but also very successful homepage. This one belongs to Quaker Marine (Quakermarine. com) – a specialty clothing store that, according to their copy, caters to those who "enjoy the grit and pleasures of the sea." Clothing for boating enthusiasts is about as small of a niche as I can imagine, yet Quaker Marine boasted a revenue of $1.3 Million in 2020. Not bad for a company with less than ten employees and only one brick and mortar location. Let's have a look at their homepage.

The first thing you see is an impeccably dressed man. He is standing in a boat with a vast blue sky behind him. This image immediately identifies not only the clothing that is for sale, but the lifestyle that is being promoted. QM's core demographic will be instantly excited by this imagery.

The only text you see reads 'End Of Season Sale.' Just below, there is a button reading 'Shop Now.'

Scroll down further. You'll see one line of copy reading 'Say hello to Quaker Marine Supply, supplier of timeless apparel for those who love the water.' Quick and to the point.

Next, we see a gallery of images. There are images of models wearing their best selling products, accompanied by links to where we can browse those products. Again, they aren't trying to make a sale. They are just showing us where we can check out more.

There is an old photograph of author Ernest Hemingway wearing one of their popular styles. This reveals more of the brand's personality. It also signifies to the shopper: "These products will make you look like a revered literary hero."

At the bottom, we find the familiar columns with links to various parts of the website – "Our Story," "Returns & Exchanges," etc.

Whereas Home Depot targets a huge demographic, Quaker Marine focuses on a very small one. With just a handful of images and a few sentences of copy, QM has made their product irresistible to anyone interested in their niche. Brilliantly done, if you ask me.

While these two companies sell very different products to very different markets, the key concepts remain the same. Establish your brand. Be as minimal as possible. Grab your customers' interest. Make it easy for them to continue shopping. Applying these principles to your homepage is a crucial step towards building a successful sales funnel, which we will discuss in depth in the following chapter.

Additional Landing Page Best Practices

– Keep The Best Stuff Above The Fold

This is a saying that harkens back to the days when nearly every adult started their day by reading an old fashioned newspaper. The newspaper itself was folded in half vertically. Editors were always trying to keep the good stuff 'above the fold,' where people would see it right away and be compelled to unfold the paper and keep reading.

These days, the printed paper is just about gone, but the concept remains the exact same. When you open a website, think of the entire screen you see at first as "above the fold." You certainly would not want to have to scroll down before you find something to grab your attention. Remember, you only have a few seconds to reel your customer in. After that, if they aren't interested, they'll be off to buy from your competition.

- Be Consistent

Consistency is a key part of establishing your brand. If you are running advertisements, make certain that you are using the same imagery and verbiage on both the ad, and the landing page. Variety can be fun, but there are other places where you can embrace that angle more effectively. The landing page should be pure, simple, and consistent with any other content you have created.

- Show Your Product In Action

Since you're probably only going to have a few images on the landing page, this is a great opportunity to show the benefits of your product right away. If you're selling baseball bats, this is a great place to include a picture of a ball player watching a home run sail off into the sky. If you are running a club for nature enthusiasts, include a picture of a group of people on an exciting rafting expedition. This is a surefire way to get visitors interested in what you have to offer.

- Include A Testimonial/Review

It is always a good thing if you can include a section featuring someone else singing your praises. Ask a satisfied client if they would be willing to give a testimonial, then place it above the fold on your landing page. This type of social proofing goes a long way towards establishing your credibility.

- Test Your Loading Time

As we've well established, this is the only chance you get to make a first impression. And these days, nothing makes a worse first impression than a slow loading time. Ideally, you need your page to be loading within 1- 2 seconds. Test this regularly. If it takes any longer to load your landing page, you're going to be losing a lot of potential sales. Be ruthless with your editing. Leave only the most essential content. There will be other opportunities to include material that requires a higher bandwidth. For now, speed is everything.

- Consider Every Device

This is a problem I run into time and time again. I see a very well designed landing page that looks great on a desktop. Then, I try to load it on my smartphone and it just doesn't translate. The text is too small, the image is hidden, I don't see a Call To Action. This is a surefire way to lose customers. Test out your landing page on iPhones, Androids, iPads, Microsoft Tablets, and anything else you think your customer might be using. Whatever item your customers are using, all the same rules apply, so do not skip this step!

Additional Case Studies

Next, I want to take a look at two extremely impressive landing pages from companies that have revolutionized their respective industries. As we study these landing pages, we will not only learn about their designs and what makes them so effective, but we will also learn about their core philosophies. The two are perfectly intertwined. Remember, your landing page is meant to tell the world who you are. All the details combine to make one powerful statement about your company and its place in the world.

Let's take a look at the start-up that has changed the hospitality industry forever.

Airbnb

For generations, hotels have had an absolute stranglehold on the hospitality industry. If you were going out of town, there was a 99% chance that you would be staying in a hotel. That is, until a company had the vision and courage to come along and change everything. Now, thanks to Airbnb (AirBNB.com), people are traveling and connecting in an entirely new way.

A company with such lofty ambitions needs to have the web operation to back it up. Otherwise, it's just another big idea. So how do they manage to pack the entire scope of their company into one little landing page? Let's break it down from top to bottom.

In the top left corner of the page, we see their now iconic logo. It is a sleek, minimalist design that appears anywhere the brand does. Great for building consistency. In the top center, we see their search bar. This is the Call To Action, the thing that invites us further into the page. It lets me easily enter my preferred destination and my dates of travel so that I can search to see what is available. In the top right, I can see a link to my own personal profile (or a link to where I create my personal profile). This is great for building relationships and familiarity with the interface.

Now let's discuss the main attraction, which is the image in the center of the page. It shows a young man standing outside of a large, well lit tent. He is camping somewhere in the middle of the desert, and you can see large stretches of nature all around him. The man himself is fit, well dressed, and offering a friendly smile and wave.

In one relatively simple image, they have done a great job of attracting the attention of their core demographic - adventurous young people who like to travel and are open to unconventional housing options. This brings me to my next point, the copy.

Underneath the image, we see their very simple, yet very effective tagline:

"Not sure where to go? Perfect."

All it takes is six words to draw you in. If I'm planning a trip, this has already excited me. Sure, I'm thinking about that serene desert from the image. But now, I'm also thinking of all the other places I could go. The California coast, New York City, Graceland, there are so many options that I feel completely compelled to answer their Call To Action and start booking my trip.

The last thing our eyes are drawn to is a neat white button underneath the tagline which reads "I'm flexible." I click on that, and I'm officially in the sales funnel. The landing page has done its job.

You'll notice that everything we have discussed so far takes place "above the fold." Let's scroll down now and see what else we can learn.

In the next frame, we see another almost irresistible call to action. This time, it is advertising Airbnb gift cards. It is a great idea, and one that many customers don't know about. So now is a perfect time for the web designers to introduce their gift cards to their core demographic.

On the left, we see the words 'Introducing Airbnb gift cards.' The lettering is big and bold, black against a white backdrop. Underneath those words, we see a button that reads 'Shop now.' It is also written in a simple black and white design which helps it to maintain consistency. Directly to the right, we see images of two actual gift cards. One of them has an image of an idyllic snowy resort town on it, which of course excites the traveler. The other one is a simple solid red design. Both of them feature the Airbnb logo, again building consistency.

Let's scroll down to the next section, which is labeled "Inspiration For Your Next Trip." This is one of my personal favorite aspects of this landing page.

There are four neatly aligned images, each one of a popular travel destination. The first panel is an advertisement for Chicago. It features a warm and inviting painting of the Chicago River, complete with huge buildings and boats lazily floating down the river. And underneath that, it shows how close it is to my current location. Very enticing!

To the right of that, I'll see three other locations, each one following the same formula as the first. They do a great job of showing the diversity of experiences that are available. From urban hotspots to dreamy lakes and mountains, they've really driven home the idea of infinite traveling options.

There are two more areas to discuss, so scroll down to the next section. We'll see two images side by side. One is labeled 'Things To Do On Your Trip,' and is accompanied by a CTA button. We see three young people on a hike inside of a scenic red dirt canyon. The people shown are diverse, which is very important for reminding potential customers that people from all walks of life are welcome.

On the right side of the page, we see another image, this one of a young woman cooking outdoors. It is labeled 'Things To Do From Home,' and accompanied by the same CTA button. This is yet another innovative idea that helps bring the spirit of connectivity to people who prefer to have their new experiences virtually.

That brings us to the last image on the page. It is a single image that takes up the entire width of the screen. It shows a woman sitting outside in a field and features the phrase "Questions about hosting?" At this point, I'm considering taking the next step and becoming a host myself. This helps to bring Airbnb's vision of a collaborative community together.

At its core, this landing page is just made up of a few simple, well placed images, and a few simple, but catchy pieces of copy. And yet, it did its job perfectly. No matter what your company is selling, I guarantee you can learn something by studying this page.

Grubhub

When I was growing up, if you wanted to order food, your best option was to find a menu, dial up your local pizza place and ask for a delivery. Then, as the internet became more and more ubiquitous in our lives, online food delivery started to creep in on their business. Now, just a few years later, thanks to a rapidly changing world, online food delivery is a constant part of our day to day lives.

There are several options out there for food delivery. But one brand in particular seems to have set the standard for all of its competitors. Grubhub became the gold standard thanks to their massive selection, easily used interface, and trustworthy delivery service. What's even more remarkable, is that people are happy to pay a higher price at Grubhub than they would by contacting a restaurant directly. Why is that?

The answer has a lot to do with their perfectly designed landing page. They've "put themselves in their customers' shoes." Who looks at Grubhub? Someone who is hungry of course! So, they load their homepage with professional photos of amazing looking meals. Once a hungry person sees all the food available to them, it is almost impossible not to place an order.

This is a unique example, because they are providing a unique service. But at its core, this landing page uses all of the same principles that make the other landing pages we have discussed so effective. Let's get right into it and see how they've utilized design and psychology to make an incredibly high converting operation.

One thing we see right away is the Grubhub logo. Like the other logos that we have studied, it is a simple two color design, and it appears on every page of the website. This subconsciously builds our trust in the brand. In the top right corner, we see our personalized options. Assuming you are signed in, you will see yourself greeted with a menu that personally greets you. If you are not signed in, you are given the option of logging in with your Facebook profile, which of course, expedites the process greatly.

Next, we come to a banner with multiple options for searches. Most landing pages would only have one search option, but because they are running a complex operation, Grubhub includes three.

In the first tab, we select when we want our food. (ASAP, 10AM tomorrow, etc).

In the second tab, we select our street address. You'll notice that they use Google Maps' auto fill feature to ensure that you can easily and accurately enter your address. Then, most importantly, you have the search bar that actually leads you to your food.

Every aspect of this search bar design is meant to keep you interested in the topic of food. They never give you the opportunity to get bored and lose interest.

When you click the food search bar, you are immediately greeted with a drop down list of 'popular searches in your area.' Pizza, Chinese, Sushi, etc. And at the very bottom of that drop down list, you'll see a list of restaurants that you have ordered from before (assuming that you are a returning customer). So now they have covered all their possible bases - customers interested in finding something new and customers looking for old favorites know that the meal they want is just a few clicks away.

Now we are going to look at my favorite part of this landing page, which I believe to be one of the reasons it is so successful. The last thing we see above the fold is a section titled 'Reorder Your Favorites.' It is a four image panel with pictures of exact meals that you have recently ordered.

Now, not only are they advertising food, they are advertising food that they already know you like. Of course, this is going to jump start your appetite! There's no turning back now, so let's keep scrolling down and see what else they have to offer.

As you scroll, notice the symmetrical design of the restaurant listings. Everything is neat and tidy, well spaced out with four restaurants per row. This allows them to pack a ton of information into a site that still loads and functions remarkably fast.

In the following rows, they show their marketing department's mastery of sales psychology. Instead of simply listing restaurants, they give each row a short category name, each one applying a slightly different tactic to encourage you to check it out.

The first row reads 'Popular Near You.' This plays into social proofing. In the same way a restaurant will get more traffic if it looks like it is busy inside, online operations get more sales if it is proven that they already have many satisfied customers. This category emphasizes restaurants with the most five star reviews. This informs your subconscious mind that these places have to be good.

The next category reads '45 Minutes Or Less.' Again, we know that the person browsing the page is hungry. There is a good chance speed is a priority. They go on to list four restaurants promising quick delivery, each one offering a different type of cuisine.

Next, we have 'National Picks.' This speaks to our inherent love of the familiar. We're given the option of ordering from Dunkin', Panera Bread, McDonald's, or any number of national chains depending on your local area. Sometimes eaters aren't feeling adventurous and just want to order an old favorite.

Finally, we come to our last

category which is titled 'Delicious Deals.' Here, the emphasis is on discounts of course, with offers like '25% off your order' and 'No delivery fee.' After all, take out can be expensive and sometimes it's nice to save a little money on your meal.

After that, we come to a section titled 'All Restaurants.' Having already been enticed by these various sales techniques, we can now either select something we have already seen or freely browse a large selection of additional restaurants.

Now, let's scroll to the bottom of the page. Here, we will find yet another key to Grubhub's success.

We see a large banner that reads 'Give the gift of food delivery.' This is an advertisement for Grubhub gift cards. Grubhub makes a large portion of their income from gift cards, and why wouldn't they? Considering that everyone has to eat, it is the perfect gift!

Finally, at the very bottom, we find the resources that Grubhub uses to build its community. After all, in order to function, they need restaurants, drivers, and customers to be willing to participate. The eyes are immediately drawn to four buttons in the right corner offering various options for restaurants and drivers who are interested in becoming a part of their operation.

Over to the left, we see even more offers. They have links to where you can sign up for Grubhub Perks, get to know their company, and connect with them on social media.
All of this content adds up to one undeniably effective home page.

Will every one of these elements be useful in your landing page? Of course not. As we study businesses both large and small, your job is to find the things that are useful to *your business.*

Conclusion

A great landing page makes a great first impression. If you employ all the tactics we have discussed above, you will inevitably start to see your conversions increase. To make sure you have covered all the most important aspects of a landing page, ask yourself the following questions:

☐ Is my brand being established right away?

_____

☐ Is this making clients want more?

_____

☐ Do I have a memorable logo?

_____

☐ Is my copy short and effective?

_____

☐ Is my page loading fast enough?

_____

☐ Is my imagery consistent?

_____

☐ Is my Call To Action clear and obvious?

_____

Chapter Four:

Getting The Most Out Of Your Sales Funnel

"There are no secrets to success. It is the result of preparation, hard work and learning from failure."
– Colin Powell

In this chapter you will learn:

- ✓ The Basic Elements Of Every Successful Sales Funnel
- ✓ How To Turn Your Client's Interest Into Action
- ✓ How To Improve Your AVO
- ✓ The Importance Of Creating Urgency

It's estimated that about 95% of eCommerce stores on Shopify eventually fail. In fact, about 80% never make a *single sale*. That isn't because they aren't selling good products (although that is sometimes the case). It's because the vast majority of people don't understand how to build a sales funnel that leads to actual conversions.

Coming up with a good idea for a product is relatively easy.

In fact, just about any idea can be made profitable with the right amount of CRO training (trust me, I've seen some really out-there products become huge sellers).

So, why do so many marketers fail?

How can you avoid common pitfalls like wasting money on advertising and simply hoping that your brand will catch on if you give it enough time?

The first thing you need to do is to completely understand the sales funnel process.

So let's start with the basics.

The sales funnel in its traditional form looks like this:

Awareness. Interest. Decision. Action.

Simple enough, right?

A customer becomes aware of a product, develops an interest, decides to purchase said product, and then takes action. The trouble, of course, is that most potential customers never get past the 'interest' stage.

For a variety of reasons that have been well documented by marketing experts, they tend to stop just short of actually typing in their credit card information. And in the rare event that they do make a purchase, the profit is barely enough to justify the money spent on advertising.

Once you've identified where your process is coming up short, you'll be well on your way to fixing it.

So be honest with yourself and try to see if any of these issues apply to you.

You may now be asking, what typically goes wrong in a sales funnel?

Here are a few of the most common errors I see.

- Poorly Designed Websites

Think about the last time you made a purchase on Amazon. Did you notice how incredibly easy it was?

You already trusted the brand, your payment information and address were already stored, you easily found what you wanted, and added the product to your cart with one click. In short, you got exactly what you wanted, extremely quickly.

For better or worse, this is the expectation of the modern consumer. We live in a world of instant gratification. For us marketers, that can be a very good thing! People are sitting at home with disposable income, eager to find some new t-shirt, e-book, or recipe that will give them a sense of excitement. But that enthusiasm can fade quickly. One broken link, one slow loading page, etc. is all it takes to turn a sale into a missed opportunity.

Look carefully at the page you've designed. Is it aesthetically pleasing? Have you compared its loading time to your competitors? Have you designed a user experience that is fun, interactive, and engaging? We'll be getting very in-depth on the topic of web design later, but for now, just start to notice areas where you can improve.

- Boring Copy

Copy is an excellent opportunity to bring your customer to that elusive second phase of the funnel: *Interest*.

Language is a powerful tool. Great copywriting taps into customers' emotions, excites them, and makes them want to spend their money. Which of the following product descriptions do you think is more likely to make a sale:

"This is a very comfortable, good looking red t-shirt. Fits all body types."

Or

"Our best-selling, fan-favorite, ruby red t-shirt is back just in time for the summer season! See why men and women across the country are ditching their stiff old tees and embracing the freedom and comfort of Sarah's T-Shirt Company."

The first example may be factually accurate, and it shares important information, but it doesn't make the customer feel anything. It just tells them that there is a red shirt that fits. Whoopee.

Now consider the second example. It establishes social proof by calling the shirt a "best-selling fan-favorite." That makes a customer feel like they are part of something. The ad says that the shirt is back 'just in time for summer.' This gives it an aura of scarcity, subconsciously telling the customer they should make this purchase soon. It emphasizes how the shirt makes you feel: comfortable and free. That is the type of copy that sells. Is it hyperbolic? Maybe a little. But it's not boring. And in copywriting, nothing is worse than being boring.

Take a look at your product descriptions. Be honest, would you get excited about that product? If not, it's time to level up your copy game. Focus on your customers' feelings, what they want, what improvements your product will make to their lives. Do this right, and your sales will go through the roof.

Note: You don't need to spend years studying copywriting to master this skill. There are ample amounts of free copywriting lessons online. But if you're pressed for time, you can always consider hiring a freelancer, or reaching out to my professional team at CROProfits.com/call

Not Enough Content

Let's say an ambitious young entrepreneur named Joe wants to start a digital wellness company. He's fit, understands nutrition and exercise, and he has correctly recognized a growing market for at home fitness programs. He decides to make a website advertising his services. He publishes his credentials, a few pictures of himself, and a list of all the services he offers. He even spends a few hundred dollars on Facebook advertising. After all, all he needs is a few clients to make that hundred dollars back. He gets his sales page set up, hits publish and then....crickets.

Joe doesn't make a single sale. Instead of getting frustrated, he decides to check out his competition (something that you should always be doing). So he looks up a successful online personal trainer, Laura, who works in his niche.

Laura's website is a goldmine of fitness information. There are daily blogs with suggested recipes, workout ideas, and fun anecdotes. Her clients post testimonials, eagerly espousing how great it has been to work with Laura. She sends out a weekly newsletter to share her recent successes. She has created a Facebook group where her clients have formed their own fitness related community.

You've probably heard of Search Engine Optimization (the process by which Google and others determine search rankings). Well, SEO *loves* webpages like Laura's. It is highly active, encourages people to interact with each other, and creates high quality content on a daily basis. When someone searches for an online personal trainer, Laura is definitely going to be high in the rankings. Her awareness is high, she has plenty of content to generate interest, and her sleekly designed webpage makes it easy for her clients to make a purchase.

Unfortunately for Joe, SEO could care less about his page. Just a few little articles, no engagement, no social media presence. He isn't going to build any awareness, much less interest. Until takes control of his SEO game, Joe is going to sink to the bottom of any search result ocean floor.

Now, look at your website. Are you a Joe or a Laura?

Getting From Interest To Decision

As we've established, most sales funnels get stuck at either awareness or interest. Customers find the page, may even develop a slight interest, but they never decide to actually spend their money. Getting from interest to decision is probably the most difficult aspect of building a successful sales funnel. Here are a few positive things you can do to dramatically increase your chance of pulling it off.

Targeting and Retargeting Your Audience.

Thanks to platforms like Facebook, putting your product in front of a targeted audience is easier than ever. But simply putting your ad in their newsfeed isn't enough. There's too much information out there, and it is exceptionally difficult to turn someone into a paying customer using just targeted Facebook ads.

Studies show that a product needs to be seen anywhere from five to twenty five times before someone is inclined to purchase it. That one ad they see might draw them to your website, but it's almost never enough to compel them to buy.

That's where retargeting comes in.

Have you ever noticed how your Instagram feed is filled with ads for products you've recently viewed? That means you are being retargeted. By visiting that organic candle website, you've identified yourself as a person interested in candles. The candle store then used what is called 'Pixel Retargeting' to put that same product back in front of your eyes. Maybe you weren't ready to purchase it right away, but after seeing it in your feed a dozen times over the next week, you'll be much more likely to complete the transaction.

Time Sensitive Offers

"50% off if you order in the next 24 hours!"

"Available for a limited time only!"

"The first twenty callers get twice the product for no additional cost!"

You've probably heard offers like this in advertising so frequently that they've become something of a cliche. But the truth is, they do work! If someone is on the fence, sometimes all they need is a little sense of urgency to make up their mind.

Direct Communication

This one is particularly important if you are offering personalized services. Many people will be hesitant to spend until they've had a direct conversation with you. So make yourself available! It is easy to put a contact form on any page of your website. Respond quickly and enthusiastically. Remember, the longer you take to respond, the more time they have to research your competition.

Free Trial (If Applicable)

If you have faith in your product, you should absolutely consider offering free trials (or 25% off the first week of your subscription etc).

Mentally, accepting a free trial feels like making a purchase. They've already committed to spending time with your product. This will make them much more likely to push your traffic over the edge to convert.

Additional Sales Funnel Best Practices

- Create Lead Magnets

A lead magnet involves giving away something for free (i.e. access to special promotions) in exchange for your customer's email address. Since we know that most clients won't be making a purchase the first time they visit, an email list is a great way to stay in touch with them and remind them that you exist. I personally am subscribed to dozens of email lists, and I can't tell you how many times I've made a purchase I otherwise wouldn't have because of an email. For example, if you are running a gym, you could offer free access to a series of advanced exercise videos in return for your client's contact information. This is mutually beneficial, and helps to build a relationship. By giving you their email address, they are telling you that they want to stay in contact. And the fact that they are willing to do so if they are given high quality content means they are already interested in what you are selling.

– Put Time And Care Into Your emails

Don't make your clients regret signing up for your email list. Above all, make sure they know that you *value their time.* Having direct access to your customers is a privilege, one that they will revoke if you don't respect them. Find an appropriate balance in regards to the frequency of your messages. Multiple emails a day will probably irritate them and lead to their unsubscribing. Let weeks go by between communications, and they will likely forget that you exist at all. Put yourself in your clients' shoes. How often do you think you would want to be contacted? That will give you your answer.

– Optimize Your Frontend

The frontend should be thought of as the very first place where a customer becomes aware of your existence. For most of us, the landing page will be the frontend of our sales funnel. You could also think of your advertisements or social media posts as a frontend. Make sure you always have a visible call to action. Without that, the process ends before it even has a chance to begin.

– Order Bumps

Have you ever wondered why grocery stores place racks of low priced items in the checkout lane? It is because the customer has already chosen to make a purchase, and now, they are much more likely to say "what the heck, I'll grab a Snickers bar too."

It must be a highly effective technique considering it is employed at thousands of stores across the country.

And yet, I rarely see digital marketers embracing this opportunity. Think of an order bump as the checkout lane - the very end of the process, when you already have your credit card in your hand. What better time to offer a few little extra products?

Amazon Fresh, Amazon's burgeoning grocery delivery service does a terrific job of encouraging extra purchases at the end of their funnel. For example, if they see that you have bread, ham, and cheese in your cart, they will suggest you add a jar of mustard or a bag of chips for only a few dollars more. I end up adding a few more products almost every time I place an order.

Remember, this is not the time to try to double your profit. Just gently suggest a few small add-ons. For example, if you buy a jersey from your favorite sports teams' store, you might be asked if you want to add a

keychain to your purchase for just ninety nine cents. You just spent ninety nine dollars, so why not!

You might also consider offering free shipping on orders of a certain amount. For example, if orders over fifty dollars ship free and I have forty dollars worth of goods in my cart, that gives me a pretty good incentive to go ahead and add at least one more item to my cart. All these little purchases add up and make a big difference to your bottom line!

Entertain, Educate, and Intrigue Your Customer At Every Step

From the beginning to the middle to the end, every single step in your customer's sales journey needs to be entertaining, educational, or intriguing. Many people make the mistake of focusing exclusively on the frontend and assuming that will be enough to sustain them through the entire process. Nothing could be further from the truth. As we have discussed, getting someone's attention with a good landing page or advertisement is only the beginning of the battle. Every step they take from their needs to be just as engaging. In the following chapters, we will hone in on both the middle and the end of the sales funnel, which will be your product pages, checkout pages, etc.

Consider Testing With Paid Traffic

We will do a deep dive into this topic later on, but now is a great time to start considering running some tests. A great way to do this is to hire a paid visitor to your page and have them make a purchase. You'll quickly be able to see how effectively your page is running. This will also reveal any possible design errors or broken links, which will of course, ruin any chance you have of boosting your conversions.

Conclusion

Your sales funnel should be in your mind at all times. When you are designing any element of your page, ask yourself if it is contributing to funnel - is it creating more conversions? Or is it just there for decoration? Your sales funnel needs to be airtight, so if you have an element on your page that isn't contributing, get rid of it. This kind of thinking might feel foreign at first, but it will put you in the mindset you need to be in to boost your conversions. Here are a few important questions to ask yourself:

☐ Do I understand all four basic elements of a traditional sales funnel?

☐ Is my content entertaining, educational, and intriguing?

☐ Have I created a sense of urgency?

☐ Is any of my content wasting my customers' time?

☐ Have I carefully considered my email strategy?

Chapter Five:

How To Create A Perfect Product Sales Page

"Copy should be long enough to do its job effectively, and not a word longer."
- Dan Kennedy

In this chapter you will learn:

- ✓ The Purpose Of A Product Page

- ✓ An Detailed Strategy For Effective Copy

- ✓ The Basics Of A/B Testing

- ✓ The Importance Of Page Loading Speed

- ✓ How To Use Powerful Words For Maximum Effect

While landing pages aren't always required, a well designed product sales page always is. Let's take an in-depth look at this important step in the sales funnel process.

The Sales Product Page is the page where your customer will look solely at the product they are considering, free from distraction. This is where you 'make' the sale. A well designed product page will have your items flying off the shelf. A poorly designed page will send your customers to the competition.

So what makes a perfect product sales page that converts with a high success rate? There are a few key ingredients. First, you need an aesthetically pleasing visual representation of your product. Next, you need a concise, compelling copy to seal the deal. In the meantime, you will need to have tested various elements of the page to find what makes your customers tick.

Making A Good Impression Right Away

Human beings are visual creatures. Keep this in mind as you design your page. Based on the image(s) you choose, a viewer will get an impression of your product almost immediately. So do not take this lightly. Hire a product photographer if you need to. Think about your ideal client, and imagine what they would like to see.

If your niche is health & wellness, feature a fit-looking model using your product. If you are selling upscale gentlemen's wear, hire an attractive man to model your product. Remember, you are appealing to the customer's subconscious desire. Use this opportunity to show how your product can improve their life.

Clean, Concise Copy

Advertising icon David Ogilvy is quoted as saying "Good copy should be easier to read than ignore." Here are some key points to keep in mind when writing your product copy:

- Keep It Short

There is a time and place for long form copy, but a product page is not it. Two to three sentences will work just fine.

- Use Everyday Language

Try reading your copy out loud. Does it sound like something you would say naturally? If not, try redoing it. People like copy that uses short sentences and small words that they easily understand.

- Use Powerful Words

There is a reason you see words like 'Amazing' in so many advertisements. Words like these sell. People would rather have an 'Amazing' experience than a 'good' experience. If you're confident in your product, don't be afraid to boast about it.

For more subtle product offerings, consider words that evoke the feeling your product is meant to create. If you are selling candles, consider 'relaxing,' 'soothing,' 'comforting,' etc. If you are selling fine wine, try 'elegant,' 'sophisticated,' etc. Always adjust your language to suit your audience.

Product Reviews

A handful of good product reviews can make all the difference in the world when it comes to closing a sale. No matter how well you market your product, there is no substitute for an endorsement from a fellow customer. So, display your five star reviews prominently. If you haven't received any reviews yet, consider offers such as 50% off your next purchase if you leave a testimonial.

Additional Visual Content

Sometimes it's hard to do your product justice using just still images. If you're selling a bicycle, an exercise routine, or anything else that involves motion, consider including some high quality video content. Show your product in action so that the client can fully understand what will be received. Other options include slideshows, diagrams, blueprints, or anything else that provides important in depth knowledge.

The Importance of A/B Testing

A/B testing (sometimes referred to as split testing), is the best way to confirm that you have made the right decisions. It takes all the guesswork out of your page design by giving you indisputable data.

Nearly every aspect of your product page should be A/B tested. There are a number of ways to do this. You can do it manually, by running one version of a product page for a fixed period of time, changing one aspect (ie the product image,) then running the new version for the same period of time. Shopify, for example, allows you to monitor your views and conversions in real time, which will show you which version is more effective.

If you know how to code, Shopify Plus gives you the option of sending different users to different variations of a product page and monitoring which performs better. This method is time consuming and requires technical proficiency, but can be very effective.

If you want to maximize the effectiveness of your A/B testing, consider hiring us by scheduling a call here: CROProfits.com/call We can do all the difficult work for you and have seen businesses make huge leaps in conversion rates after testing the smallest details of a page, often things that most business owners don't even consider.

Pricing In Regards To A/B Testing

Determining the correct price point is difficult. If the price is too low, your customer might assume the product is low quality. If it is too high, they might look for a more affordable alternative. Then, there are countless variables to consider. IE: Why do products that cost $9.99 sell better than products that cost $9.95?

You have two choices when it comes to setting a price point: Take a guess, or meticulously split test until you have found an effective, data-based solution. You can probably guess which method I recommend.

Page Speed

I've emphasized minimalism on product pages for good reason. You need your product page to load *quickly*. It's a fast paced market place, and no one wants to wait around for 20 seconds while your page loads. Keeping images and videos to a minimum will help your page load instantly, not giving your clients a chance to lose interest.

A Story About Page Speed

This seems like a great opportunity to tell a story about how I used my knowledge of page speed analytics alone to boost a company's revenue **10X**. If you weren't already convinced of page speed's importance, I guarantee you will be after hearing this.

When I was working with one of my larger clients, they were experiencing major struggles at the checkout point in the funnel and seeing a big drop-off in sales. Everything about the website seemed to be in tip-top shape, so naturally, they were perplexed and desperate to find a solution to their problem.

So, I did what I always do - I started testing. And I pretty quickly realized the problem - their page was loading at five times the speed of their competitors. Worse still, their load times on mobile devices were just abysmal. I brought my findings to upper management, but

they dismissed my concerns right away. They said the page loaded "fast enough," and that I needed to keep looking for the real issue.

But my mind was already made up. I knew I would have to prove to them that page speed was indeed the problem. And what better way is there to do that than to present cold, hard, indisputable data. So I got to work and started doing my own research.

The statistics I came up with were downright shocking. I almost couldn't believe the numbers, but every test I did further confirmed my discovery:

For every one second your page is delayed in loading, it loses 7% of its possible revenue.

That means that if your website has an average income of $100K per day, you could be *losing two and a half million dollars per year!* Just for being one second slower than the competition.

When I presented these facts

to management, they changed their tune pretty quickly. I also gave them some specific details about what might be slowing them down – lost pages, broken links, etc. Once they saw how much money they were losing because of these very fixable problems, improving page speed became priority number one.

So we started working together to create a plan of action. We identified which specific pages were loading the slowest. We found areas where outdated technology was still being implemented. We found images that hadn't been properly compressed, leading to excessive load times. It was a very detail oriented process, which involved me working with their team of developers very closely. (You may not have the resources of this large company, but don't let it stop you from hiring a freelance developer if you need to!)

So together, we created a highly effective speed optimization plan. This was a few years back, so we had to do a lot of testing manually. These days, there are tons of tools and resources you can use to test load times, and the experts are very good at improving it!

As you might have guessed, once our work was done, the company's profits soared. It was one of my first projects that led to a **10X** increase in conversions, but it certainly wasn't the last! Since then, I've known to make this an essential part of my process. Every split second you shave off your loading times will increase your conversion rate – and your bottom line.

Product Page Case Studies

Pilgrim

Pilgrim is consistently one of the top performing stores on Shopify. They are an aromatherapy outlet, selling a wide variety of diffusers and oils. Let's go to PilgrimCollection.com and check out what their product pages look like.

For this example, I am going to focus on their 'Disconnect' Collection.

When I open the product page, I am immediately greeted by a minimalist design with one image of the product for sale. It is a package of diffusible oils with names like 'Sweet Orange' and 'Frankincense.' Considering that this product is meant to help people 'disconnect' from their busy lives, they've done a great job of appealing to their niche right away.

They have included a scroll bar for the images, which helps the page maintain its fast loading time while still offering a variety of things to look at. As we scroll through the images, we see flowers, clean sheets, a smiling mother with her children. The message here is that 'You too could be a happier, more effective parent if you took the time to treat yourself with our relaxing scents.'

Now let's look at the copy:

"Meant to help **relieve stress**, this oil collection enables **deep mind & body relaxation**."

This one short sentence is all they need. Notice the words they've chosen to put in bold. It is easy to read and promises something we all need. Incredibly effective.

This product page also makes it very easy to move on to the checkout page. There are several buttons indicating accepted payment methods (ShopPay, PayPal etc.). Click on 'Add To Cart,' and within one second you are given the option to check out. Note the emphasis on speed and efficiency. Nothing can be more important!

REI

Next, let's take a look at a very different, but equally effective product page. This time, we're going to check out the outdoor megastore, REI.com.

Let's pick out an item that includes a lot of technical specifications to see how that alters the product page design. For our purposes, we're going to select a pair of binoculars. I enter 'binoculars' in the search bar, and immediately, I see plenty of options. Let's select the first option - the 'Nikon Prostaff 3S'

The page loads very quickly, which as we've established, is everything. And yet, there is still plenty of information packed onto this page. The developers must have done a great job of using compressed, fast loading imagery.

Binocular design tends to be very detailed, so if I'm going to make a purchase, I'm going to need to get a good, up-close view. Fortunately, I have instant access to five different angles. Notice that only one image is full sized at a time. This helps keep my focus, and keeps page speeds high.

My eye is immediately drawn to the item's 50+ five star reviews. Social proofing, as we know, is huge. There is a button that reads 'Top Rated.' Knowing that this item is endorsed by such a well respected company gives me a lot of confidence. And I even see that this item comes with free shipping. Lots of incentive to buy here! But this isn't some impulse purchase. I'm going to need to learn a lot more about these binoculars before I'm willing to pull the trigger. So let's scroll down and see what we find beneath the fold.

The first line of copy I see reads:

"**Waterproof**, fog proof, and **built tough** for the **outdoors**, the Nikon Prostaff 3S 10x42 binoculars boast an **advanced optical system** for sharp images that bring the **far away up close**.

This is a great piece of copy. While it doesn't speak to the layman, to someone interested in binoculars, it is extremely appealing. Look at the words I've chosen to highlight for emphasis. They clearly appeal to the budding outdoors enthusiast. These words inspire a sense of adventure, which is, of course, a great example of a marketer knowing their audience. Take specific note of the last four words – "Far away up close" – That is a terrific tagline. It is short and effective, while still being extremely specific to the product. Very well done.

Now let's check out the "Features" section. There are eight bullet points, each one explaining a little bit more about what makes this pair of binoculars special. The first bullet point reads like this:

"These full-size binoculars offer a **steady view**, ideal for use on boats and for **serious wildlife viewing**."

The words I've emphasized reassure me that these are for people who are serious about looking at wildlife. They are not toys. It also ignites my imagination, by making me think about boats and nature. That feeling of excitement gets me a little closer to making a purchase.

"Highly reflective, **silver alloy mirror coating** gives you a bright and clear view."

You'll notice that as we get further down the list, we get away from general language and into more and more specifics. It is assumed that if I am still reading at this point, then I am very willing to go into details.

We also see a chart that shows every specification I could imagine. Now I'm hooked. I've seen everything I need to see, I've been educated, and I'm excited about the opportunity for adventure that comes with these binoculars. I click 'add to cart,' and we're off to check out!

Conclusion

There is so much to learn from studying product pages. Let the ideas we've discussed here serve as inspiration while you do your own research. Find the product page for something you are interested in and break it down to the littlest detail. What touches your emotions? What excites you? How are you being educated? Don't be afraid to copy ideas that you like. You'll always find something new.

Before moving on to the next step in your sales funnel, ask yourself the following questions:

☐ Is my product page clean and attractive?

☐ Am I using high quality images?

☐ Am I using powerful language that excites my customers?

☐ Am I using intelligent language that educates my customer?

☐ Are my customers having an emotional response to my content?

☐ Is it easy to get from the product page to the checkout page?

Chapter Six:

Seal The Deal With An Effective Checkout Page

"Success is often achieved by those who don't know that failure is inevitable."
– Coco Chanel

In this chapter, you will:

- ✓ Learn The Secrets Of Crafting an Effective Checkout Page

- ✓ Understand The Three Core Elements Every Checkout Page Needs

- ✓ Learn Why Customers Abandon Checkouts (And How To Avoid It)

- ✓ Continue Building Relationships After The Transaction Is Complete

We've finally arrived at the last step of your sales funnel – the checkout page. This is where they enter their credit card or crypto information, press 'Finalize,' and most importantly, you get paid.

Many amateur marketers don't put too much stock into their checkout page. After all, the customer has already taken the time to explore the website and selected a product to purchase. What could possibly go wrong from here?

The answer is 'a lot.'

The checkout page is just as important as your landing and product pages. There's nothing worse than seeing that a customer made it all the way to this step of the process only to abandon their order. In this chapter, we're going to show you how to make sure that doesn't happen.

There are three key elements to focus on.

- – Ease

- – Speed

- – Trust

If you utilize these three concepts, your customers will happily come back to you time and time again. Ignore them at your own peril.

Ease

eCommerce giants like Amazon have poured hundreds of millions of dollars into perfecting their checkout process. They have studied every little detail en route to finding out exactly what checking out should look and feel like. When you log into Amazon, your payment information and delivery address are already saved. You can purchase items with a single click. And in many cases, you can have your items delivered within 24 hours.

You may not have the resources to run your store like Amazon, but you should still learn from their example. Later in the chapter, we will explore specific ideas on how to make your checkout process as easy as possible.

Speed

The checkout page needs to be lightning fast. Every second spent waiting for the page to load is an opportunity for your customer to change their mind. Streamline the process as much as possible. More on this to come.

Trust

This is perhaps the most important element. People are more weary of cyber crime than ever before. They are hesitant to enter their personal information on a new website for the first time. You and I know that most online transactions are extremely safe. But your customer may not. Your job is to reassure them.

The easiest way to ensure your client's safety is to install the most up-to-date 256 bit encryption SSL Certificate on your website. Most hosts offer this service for free, however, a paid version that offers enhanced security and peace of mind is also available. Displaying your SSL Certificate prominently on your checkout page will further boost conversions and discourage customers from bouncing away.

Shopify makes it easy for you to accept trusted payment options like GooglePay, ApplePay, etc. Prominently featuring these logos is a great way to instantly build trust and familiarity.

The sports apparel company Fanatics.com refers to their checkout page as 'Secure Checkout.' It features the logos of well-known brands they accept, such as Visa, Discover, etc. It prominently advertises free shipping on orders over $24, as well as a generous return/exchange policy. All of these things combine to instantly build trust.

Specific Strategies To Implement Into Your Checkout Page

- Accept As Many Types Of Payment As Possible

Personally, I use PayPal at every opportunity. I have multiple credit cards saved, and I can easily choose which one I want to use for each specific purchase. Some people are loyal Apple customers who prefer to use ApplePay. And some older customers have yet to embrace these methods.

As we blast into the future, apps are also now readily available to accept crypto payments such as Bitcoin, further expanding the audience and ability for your customers to purchase from you.

The fact is, every payment method you exclude will lose you

customers. So accept them all!

- Make Yourself Available For Communication

It is easy to add a live chat to your checkout page. Sometimes answering a quick question can be the difference between a sale and an abandoned checkout.

- Allow Guest Checkout

Of course, you want to sign people up to your website so you can add them to your mailing list, stay in touch, etc. But you should never make it mandatory. Always allow for guest checkout - hopefully your customer will enjoy their experience enough to come back and become a member.

- Enable Social Sign In

We're always trying to eliminate steps and expedite the process. If applicable to your service, consider allowing social sign in. This means that instead of creating a new account, users can simply use Facebook to confirm their identity. This may not be relevant to everyone, but to certain businesses, it is a very helpful way of making things easier on your client.

- Don't Neglect Mobile Design

Everyone loves shopping from their phone! Make sure you have optimized your mobile design so that customers can make a quick purchase during their downtime at work, their commute, etc. Double check the look and feel from various devices and have colleagues, friends, and family do the same to provide you with a good range of helpful fixes from their feedback.

- Increase Your Average Order Value

Increasing your Average Order Value (AOV) is a very important metric to take into consideration when you are attempting to increase your conversions. Remember those $.99 candy bars displayed at the checkout aisle in a grocery store. If you have any low priced items, consider making it easy to add them to the order before final checkout. Your customer has already decided that they are going to spend their money, it can't hurt to offer a little more!

Tricks To Avoid Shopping Cart Abandonment

If you're seeing a lot of customers leaving items in their cart without making a purchase, you're not alone. Statistics vary, but it is estimated that as many as seven out of ten customers who make it to your checkout page never actually complete their purchase. That number is even higher for the ever growing number of people who shop on mobile devices. But there are a few little tricks you can employ that might help your customers break through the last barrier.

- Be Upfront About Cost

As a consumer, very little is as frustrating as a last second fee. If a product I am interested in is advertised to me at $19.99, that's what I want to pay. Adding last second fees for any reason is likely to turn me away. There was a time where this type of practice was accepted, but customers have become very weary of it over the last few years. Your checkout page should clearly list your price, with no last second surprises.

- Only Ask For Essential Information

Of course, you want to learn more about your customer, but now is not the time for that. You need their email address, payment info, and shipping address. Anything else just slows down the process and makes it more likely that they leave without finishing their purchase.

- "Are You Sure You Want To Leave Without Completing Your Order?"

Creating an exit pop-up can be a good last ditch effort. Maybe use this opportunity to offer a small discount, or some other benefit. It won't work every time, but it won't hurt to try!

- Enable Form Field Validation

Inserting real time form field validation can prevent customers from things like misspelled addresses or inaccurate information. This automatically eliminates the potential for misunderstandings or botched orders.

- Follow Up emails and Texts

Just because they aren't making a purchase today, that doesn't mean they might not come back. Sending a potential customer a follow up to see if they are still interested can be a great way of turning a lost sale into a conversion. There is much more to come on this in future chapters.

- Autosave Contents Of Cart

Hopefully, your customer will return to your page after being successfully retargeted. Or maybe they'll make the decision on their own! Either way, if their items are right where they left them, that speeds up the process of them finally completing that elusive sale.

Every one of these elements should be thoroughly tested and retested. If you're pressed for time, consider checking out the services we offer by jumping on a call with us: CROProfits.com/call We've designed and tweaked 1000's of checkout pages, and we'd be happy to make you our next best success story!

After The Sale

Hopefully, your fully optimized checkout page is starting to give you a tangible improvement in your conversions. This is where the real fun (and the real profit) starts. Make sure you have an automated confirmation sent to their email right away. This will show that you're trustworthy and build excitement for the incoming item. Use a tracking app like Shop to give them access to real time information about the whereabouts of their package.

Now that you've made a sale, you can start focusing on turning that one-time customer into a repeat customer. Reach back out to make sure that they are satisfied with their purchase. Ask them to share a positive testimonial in return for a discount on their next offer. Consider giving them a shout out on social media if it is appropriate.

Case Study

We're going to take a look at the extremely successful online furniture outlet Wayfair.com. This is a company that regularly reports revenue in the millions. That means that not only are they getting tons of traffic, but that traffic is following the sales funnel all the way to end. I want to emphasize the ease of the process. I also want to point out the reassuring features that make me willing to spend hundreds, even thousands of dollars here. I'll pick an item at random and follow the full check out process.

Each product page has an attractive purple button reading 'Add To Cart.' As soon as I click it, I am greeted by a pop-up window within milliseconds. It is titled 'Add Protection, Enjoy Peace Of Mind.' Here, I am given the option to ensure my purchase. I can easily scroll through insurance options. For example, I can select something like '3 year protection plan for $11.99.' It is a great chance for them to improve their AVO, and it also encourages me to continue the process without having to worry about my item breaking. Furthermore, the 'Allstate' Insurance logo is included. I'm already made to feel very comfortable.

I select the insurance package I'd like and continue. A checkout menu comes up on the right side of the screen. At the top, we see a purple button placed in the right corner. It is the same font as every other button, which helps build a good sense of consistency. I see everything I need to know about my order, a picture of the item, its individual price, and the subtotal of my cart. I also see the phrase 'This Order Ships Free!" I know exactly what to expect. And of course, they've suggested a pillow that goes well with the couch I'm ordering.

I happen to have an account here, so as soon as I proceed, all of my information is already saved. Wisely, they include the option of checking out as a guest as well. Of course, they have my credit card numbers, but they also have several other payment options. I can get 5% off my order if I sign up for a Wayfair Credit Card. I can use Afterpay or Klarna to make my payment interest free in four installments over the next two months. And of course, I have more familiar options like PayPal to choose from as well.

From there, everything is simple. The next click takes me to my review page where I confirm all my information. One more click, and my order is complete.

Conclusion:

We have now established exactly what a sales funnel is, how to build one, what to put in it, and in this chapter, how to effectively seal the deal. It certainly isn't easy, but it's an incredibly rewarding process. In the following chapters, we will delve deeper into specific marketing techniques, sales philosophies, and advanced concepts. For now, take all the time you need to master your checkout page. Once you're feeling confident, ask yourself these questions, then feel free to move on to the next chapter.

☐ Is my checkout page fast, easy, and efficient?

☐ Am I accepting every payment method?

☐ Have I established my credibility using trust seals?

☐ Have I enabled guest checkout?

☐ Am I prepared to continue building relationships after the checkout process is complete?

Chapter Seven:

Why Category Pages Are Vital To Any Website

"Yesterday's home runs don't win today's games."
– Babe Ruth

In this chapter, you will learn:

- ✓ How Category Pages Provide a Smooth Shopping Experience

- ✓ How Category Pages Can Boost Your SEO Results

- ✓ Different Strategies For Organizing Your Content

- ✓ How To Get The Most Out Of Your In-Site Search Engine

- ✓ Effective Strategies For Writing Long-Form Copy

Next, I would like to focus on another often overlooked topic - category pages (often referred to as Product Listing Pages). Category pages have two distinctive purposes. First, they allow visitors to narrow down their search and see the different options you offer related to their specific interests. Second, category pages play an important role in your page's SEO results. In this chapter, we will view several exceptionally designed category pages to see what we can learn from them.

Utilizing Category Pages To Optimize User Experience

Properly designed category pages create a smooth journey from interest to action. A visitor should be able to come to your site with a general need - a sweater for example - and quickly find the exact thing they need - say, a blue, fleece, hoodie.

For our first example, we are going to look at the popular department store, Kohls.com. Kohl's provides a great blueprint for stores that offer hundreds of different products. Despite their huge inventory, it is easy to find exactly what you want (and perhaps discover something you didn't know you wanted).

First, we're going to visit the homepage. Then, we're going to click on 'Shop By Department', which is prominently featured at the top of the page. A vertical menu will appear. We see general categories, such as 'Men's,' 'Bed & Bath' etc. We also see specialized categories such as 'Women's Plus Size' and 'Baby.' No need to waste time scrolling through endless, vague categories, we can find exactly what we want right away. For our purposes, let's select 'Men.'

The 'Men's' page packs in an incredible amount of information, yet it is not in any way overwhelming. It achieves this by offering several simple ways of categorizing our search. For example, we have the option to:

- Shop New Brands

- Shop By Size

- Shop By Category

All of these appear in a neatly organized vertical menu on the left side of the page.

In the center of the page, we see more specific categories - Athletic, Jeans & Pants, Jackets, and Outerwear. Each of these is accompanied by a bright, high quality image of a model wearing the respective item.

Within a few seconds, we've been shown that this store offers high quality products. We've also been shown exactly how to find them.

Let's continue our hypothetical search for a new sweater by clicking on 'Hoodies and Sweatshirts.'

On the following page, I am immediately greeted by five thumbnail sized images showcasing the five most popular types of sweaters - Active, Fleece, Big & Tall, Crewneck, and Sports Fan.

On the left, there is a scroll down menu allowing me to choose by color.

I'm going to select fleece.

Even after all that narrowing down, there are still thousands of options for me to choose from. Fortunately, this flawless design makes it easy for me to continue sorting until I find exactly what I want.

Above the product listings, we'll see a 'Sort By' option. This device has become ubiquitous in eCommerce, so make sure you have one.

Let's say I'm on a budget, so I select 'Sort By Price - Low To High.'

The first thing I see is a nice, affordable fleece sweater. And what do you know, it happens to come in blue.

In less than a minute, I was able to find exactly what I was after at a price that I could afford. I click on the product page and make my purchase.

Getting The Most Out Of Your In-Site Search Engine

Our next example is particularly relevant for smaller stores who sell more specialized products. We're also going to focus on the in-site search engine - a critical tool for helping users find highly specific products. It is also extremely helpful for your SEO results - more on that later.

For this example, we are going to look at Foxtrotco. com.

Foxtrot separates itself from standard food and grocery stores by offering a curated selection of top quality specialty foods from small, local businesses. For people with dietary restrictions - vegan, gluten- free etc.- companies like this are a godsend. But only if you can find what you're looking for. Let's check out the site and see how that search engine works.

In the top right corner of the sleek, minimalist landing page, I see a search bar. Let's say I came here because I am a vegan and having trouble finding food I like. I enter 'Vegan' and I am immediately greeted by dozens more products. They arrive on a neatly organized grid. Suddenly it feels like I am shopping in a specialized section of the store, just for me. No more wondering what items fit my diet, I know that everything is good. I can repeat this using any other dietary phrase – 'gluten free,' 'keto,' or even just 'healthy.'

Foxtrot's search engine also has another great function. After you enter your initial search, you will see a list of 'Popular Searches' underneath the search bar. Categories including 'Pinot Noir,' 'Meals,' 'Salads,' etc. are all just one click away. Now not only have I found what I wanted, I've been given the opportunity to see other top quality foods that I might be interested in. No wonder people spend money hand over fist here (Foxtrot reported a revenue of over $100M in 2021).

Luring Customers In With Long Form Copy

Up until now, we've put a strong emphasis on short, punchy copy. Your category page, on the other hand, gives you the perfect opportunity to test out some long form copy. This is especially effective for stores that cater to hobbyists – passionate people with disposable income who are interested in learning about and acquiring the best toys and gadgets.

For this case study, we're going to check out Sweetwater – one of the biggest online distributors of musical instruments and equipment in the country – and a company that makes over $800M a year.

Go to Sweetwater.com. Directly under their logo, you'll see a drop down menu which reads 'Shop By Category.' From there, we can hover over the appropriate category and see its subsequent subcategories. Let's select 'Guitars' as our main category,' and 'Electric Guitars' as our subcategory.

Right away, we're going to see more content than we usually see on a product page or landing page.

The headline here reads: "Choose Your Next Electric Guitar With Caution." It is followed by a detailed description of how the company ensures that your guitar will be delivered in impeccable condition - a critical thing for a company that sells guitars for up to $10K. (Refer back to the "Trust" section in Chapter 6)

This large section of copy is broken up by several product grids - (more on that to come). This keeps the reader from becoming overwhelmed by excessive text. When we scroll to the bottom, however, we find several hundred words of copy, each paragraph describing one of the subcategories of electric guitars. Let's take a look at the opening paragraph. It reads:

"If you're looking to purchase a new electric guitar, **congratulations**! You've come to the right place. Whether you want the **low-tuned rumble** of an extended-range Ibanez solid body electric guitar or the **warm jazz tones** of a classic Gibson ES hollow body electric guitar, Sweetwater has a **massive inventory** of some of the best electric guitars to choose from. And with one of the largest teams of **guitar experts** in the industry, we're ready, willing, and able to help you find the **perfect instrument** of your dreams."

I've highlighted my favorite words and phrases from this passage to show you how you can use positive language to entice your customer.

- Congratulations

This makes the customer feel like they are in the right place. It also conveys the dealer's enthusiasm, which is a critical part of any sale.

- Low Toned Rumble, Warm Jazz Tones

If you're not a guitarist, this probably seems like gibberish. But if you are a guitarist, these phrases will immediately get you excited about how your new guitar will sound. They show that the person you are buying from is as passionate about guitars as you are.

- Massive Inventory, Guitar Experts, Perfect Instrument

More enthusiastic language makes me want to shop here. Somewhere in that massive inventory, the perfect guitar is waiting for me, and they have a team of experts available to help at any time. What more could a guitar enthusiast ask for?

This page goes on to describe further subcategories of electric guitars, and also links to expertly written articles with titles like "How To Choose Electric Guitar Strings." All this content combined gives the customer an unshakable sense of confidence and makes them willing and eager to spend their money.

A/B Test Opportunity: The length of your category page copy provides a great opportunity to split test. After a few hundred visits, try a variety of different content word lengths to see which fits best to ultimately boost your conversions. Work with your developer to show a snippet of content, followed by a 'Continue reading..' button which reveals the remaining text. This will also allow you to balance info - vs- grid of products and leaves plenty of data to further analyze for additional growth opportunities.

Note: This type of advanced conversion testing is what we do all day long at CROProfits. com/call Feel free to reach out to jump on a call with our team that will offer you specialized advice.

Product Grids

Now, let's get into a topic we have mentioned a few times throughout this chapter - Product Grids (or lists). These are the product listings that make up the bulk of visual content on any product page. As always, they feature high quality images of the product, price listing, and a link to the respective product page. It sounds simple, but there are a lot of decisions to be made. This is one of the most split testable elements of your entire store, so I encourage you to try as many designs as possible.

Here are a few key things to think about when designing your product grid:

- Products Per Row

There's no golden rule here - but a good rule of thumb is to max out around four or five images per row. This is Amazon's standard practice, as well as the formula used in most of the designs we've studied so far. There are of course exceptions. If you are selling smaller products with images that require less bandwidth, 7- 8 products per row may also be worth testing.

- Ability To Sort

As we mentioned earlier, giving your customer the option of how to sort products helps give them a smoother shopping experience. Most sorting functions default to 'Most Popular,' but make sure to include the option to sort by price. Also consider adding options specific to your product i.e. size, availability, color, etc. Try to frequently change the 'default' sorting option with the goal of continuing to boost your conversions!

- What Information To Include/Hide

In addition to an image and price, consider various tests which include showing/hiding buy buttons, star ratings, discounts, payment plans, and anything else that might pique your customer's interest.

- Mobile Optimization

Make sure that your design translates to mobile. Smaller screens means less images, and most likely a switch to one product per row, in list form. Don't miss out on those lucrative mobile sales because your product grid is too busy to be effective on an iPhone screen.

Every little change you make to your product grid has the potential to massively boost your sales. So when in doubt, test and test again.

Category Page Best Practices

- Consider That Your Product Page Might Be Your First Impression

In an ideal world, customers would always start right on your landing page and move through the funnel exactly how you designed it. But oftentimes, Search Engine Optimization results will lead your client straight to a category page. For example, if they search for Diver's Watches, and that is the name of one of the categories of your watch store, they are likely to bypass the landing page altogether.

Make sure all the key elements we introduced on your landing page are here as well. Your logo, your brand, the story, and personality you are selling - these should be key ingredients to your category pages.

– Give Your Category Pages Simple Names

Both to improve SEO results and to avoid confusing your customers, give your category pages the simplest names you can imagine. Two words is good. One word is better. This headline is not where you show off your product, just where you show what it is.

Good examples:

- Fishing Rods

- Soccer Cleats

- Headphones

Bad examples:

- Deluxe New Fishing Rods

- Super Comfortable Soccer Cleats

- Headphones With Booming Bass Sounds

– Use A Filtering System

Don't you hate it when you find the perfect shirt while browsing a clothing store only to find that they don't have it in your size? A filtering option is the perfect solution. It allows users to select a specific aspect, and then only be shown items that fit that aspect. What parameters your filter follows will vary depending on your website. NFL.com for example, allows you to filter by team, in addition to standard options like size and color.

Without filtering, you run the risk of overwhelming your clients, especially if you have a large inventory. Even worse, you could frustrate them by making it too difficult to find what they are looking for.

– Be Consistent With Image Sizes

You may be tempted to get creative by having some images larger than others. I highly recommend avoiding this, as it just makes your page look disorganized and unprofessional. Select a good size that is large enough to show the details of your product and use that throughout your category page.

- Don't Neglect Page Speed

I've made myself pretty clear about the importance of loading times on product pages. However, it is just as important that you have a fast loading product page. This can be tricky, as you are likely including more images than you would elsewhere. Work with a developer to make sure that all the images you include are compressed down to the smallest possible file size. You can still include several images, you just have to be smart about it.

Case Study For A Smaller Store Bebemoss

In our previous example, we covered a store that markets its products specifically to well educated adults using detailed, tech heavy content. In this example, we are going to look at a much smaller operation, one which takes the exact opposite approach.

Bebemoss is one of the top performing independent stores in its industry, and is consistently advertised by Shopify itself as a prime example of what can be accomplished using their platform.

They sell children's toys. By putting a twist on classic stuffed animals, they have tapped into an ever fruitful market of parents looking to provide a fun experience for their children. Needless to say, marketing these items requires an entirely different approach, more focused on visuals and emotion than technical specifications.

From the landing page, we will select 'Toys.' By using this most simple of category page names, they have informed both their visitors and the SEO algorithm what is for sale. From there, they subcategorize their stuffed animals by what part of the world they would live in ie - woodlands, ocean, etc. I'm going to select 'Safari.'

That brings us to the category page itself. First, let's start with what makes the category page similar to the previous example. As before, the branding is ubiquitous, with the logo appearing prominently in the left top corner. I have easy access to a search menu in the top right corner, and can view my cart at any time by hovering over the icon. That is about where the similarities end!

This product listing page has everything to do with visuals. Because these are children's products, the designers didn't clog up any space with unneeded copy. After all, their target demographic might not even be able to speak yet. So instead, they have emphasized the adorable products they sell.

I only have six items to choose from here, which keeps me from overthinking what should be a relatively easy purchase. They are listed in two rows of three. We only see the most essential information - what it looks like, what it is named, and how much it costs. You will also notice that each product appears against a pure white backdrop, reinforcing the minimalist appeal of this page.

This speaks to a great understanding of the brand's customers. When shopping for something simple like a toy, they are not using logic. They are thinking purely with their emotions. They want something that will make their child's eyes light up, maybe even something that reminds them of their own childhood. Any extra information removes them from that trance-like state and possibly dissuades them from making the purchase.

You will also notice that each product appears against a pure white backdrop, reinforcing the minimalist appeal of this page.

At the bottom, as per usual you'll see the standard links to blogs, FAQ's, Delivery Options, etc. All of which are designed using simple columns of text and pleasing colors to match the brand's aesthetic.

Conclusion:

Now that you have taken an in depth look at two very different, yet equally effective types of category pages, hopefully, you are starting to realize the importance of their design. You should also have gained a greater understanding of how they impact your search results. As you work on designing your own category page, you should ask yourself these questions:

☐ Are my products properly arranged and easy to browse?

☐ Have I given my categories simple, SEO friendly titles?

☐ If appropriate, have I provided educational content on what I am selling?

☐ Have I designed my listings to appeal to my core demographic?

☐ Are my designs neat and symmetrical?

☐ Is my page loading fast enough?

☐ Is my product listing page as effective on a mobile device as it is on a desktop?

Chapter Eight:

Omnipresence With Your Clients

"Do what you do so well that they will want to see it again and bring their friends."
– Walt Disney

In this chapter, you will learn:

- ✓ How To Use Different Social Media Platforms To Become a Part Of Your Customers' Lives

- ✓ Strategies For Communicating Directly To Your Customers

- ✓ How To Automate Communication

- ✓ How To Create and Implement an Effective email Strategy

- ✓ The Benefits Of Creating a Rewards Program

- ✓ How To Break Into The Lucrative Market Of Live Virtual Events

Earlier in the book, we stated that CRO is a mixture of art and science. And so far, that is what we have dealt with - we've talked about making an aesthetically pleasing website that functions efficiently and leads to more sales.

There is another, equally vital component to making a sale.

The human element.

In this chapter, we're going to discuss how you can use your personality to build long lasting relationships with your clients.

Anyone who owns a restaurant will tell you that it is easy to get a customer to come in for one meal. It is much more difficult, however, to get them to come back. As a foodie and formally trained chef, (I could write another book one day on that fun, bucket list experience) I visit restaurants frequently.

So what makes these favorite food spots this special to keep going back?

Simple. It's the atmosphere. It's the people.

When I walk in the door to my favorite joints, I am a regular on a first name basis. When seated by their team, they know what I want. The usual! When they say "Thanks for coming in, see you soon," I know they mean it. The following weekend, there's a good chance I'll be right back, seated at the same booth.

You can create these experiences with your website as well. Let's get into some specific strategies you can implement to build personal relationships and develop omnipresence with your online clients.

Social Media – Facebook and Beyond

Social media strategies could easily warrant their own chapter in this book. Here, I want to cover some core strategies that relate specifically to our goal of building omnipresence.

The moment you finish creating your Business's Facebook profile, you are immediately given access to tools that small business owners used to only dream of. Right away, you can start expanding on your brand, communicating directly with existing customers, and reaching potential customers in every corner of the world. It truly is an invaluable resource.

I've seen companies improve their conversion rate well over **10X** simply by utilizing the strategies we are about to discuss.

Let's start by pointing out some of the things that make social media such a powerful tool.

Facebook has *evened the playing field.*

It has broken down the barrier between seller and buyer.

It has given everyone the ability to be heard.

Without social media, it would be easy for companies to monopolize their respective industries, leaving no room for competition from ambitious young entrepreneurs. One would need to have an advertising budget in the millions to reach a global audience.

Now, you can do it for as little as a dollar a day.

And this business model is *infinitely scalable.*

With even the smallest budget, you can get a few small wins. From there, you can double your budget to as little as two dollars a day, and watch your conversions start to increase. Before you know it, you'll be calculating scaling your business like a seasoned pro!

As you may have guessed, it won't be easy.

But here is some good news:

Most of your competitors aren't even taking the first steps toward success on Facebook.

We're going to start with some basic elements of Facebook marketing.

If you follow these steps, you will already have a major leg up on the competition.

Facebook Basics

– Fill Out Everything

Facebook does a brilliant job of laying out what information you should share. And yet, so many businesses leave major sections of their profiles blank. Do they really think Facebook would have included these sections if they weren't important?

Whether it is a text section or an image section, every aspect of your profile is a new opportunity to show the world who you are. You don't want to be representing yourself with any blank space.

- Consistent Imagery Across Platforms

Make sure that the images you use in your Facebook profile are the same ones you are using on both your website, and any other platforms that you use. Remember, we want to become omnipresent with our clients. Brand consistency is a key element here. Seeing that same logo or picture over and over subtly reinforces the idea that you are a trusted, reliable professional.

- Properly Formatted Images

I've seen people pay good money to get professional logos designed, only to post them to their profile with the wrong dimensions. As a result, the logo comes out dull, grainy, and unprofessional looking.

If you are good with image editing, consider using a platform like Canvas. They provide the exact specifications needed for profile pictures, banners, and advertisements.

If you would rather hire a professional, there are countless freelancers who can handle this task at a very low price. Fiverr.com is just one of the freelance marketplaces you might consider browsing.

- Connect To All Your Other Pages

As we have stated before, Search Engine Optimization algorithms love seeing pages that are linked together. They are proven to keep users engaged for longer than pages that stand alone.

This applies to both your website and any existing social pages you have. Because they are both owned by Meta, it is extremely easy to link your Facebook to your Instagram. But don't forget to link to any other platforms that you regularly use (if you are interested in branching out into other platforms, we will discuss that later in the section).

- Post Regularly

Unfortunately, many people give up on their businesses much too soon (often because they don't use these techniques).

Because of that, there are thousands and thousands of Facebook business profiles that have completely stopped producing content. SEO notices this and sends them to the very bottom of any search list, probably never to be viewed again.

You need to show both your customers and the algorithms that your page is very much alive.

Keep a steady stream of content coming out at all times.

Trust me here, not posting enough is a way bigger problem than posting too much.

What To Post

With a relatively new profile, variety is key when it comes to posting. Consider this your data collecting stage. You can easily track which types of posts get the most likes and the time of day you are posting them. You can also see which posts are sending traffic to your website (the ultimate goal).

You may be tempted to post a bunch of ads for your product, but I recommend avoiding this at first.

Instead, I like to use the following model:
- One third of your content should be entertaining.

- One third of your content should be informational.

- One third of your content should be advertising your product.

Of course, this formula can be adjusted any way you please, depending on the results you get. But it is a great way to get started.

The reason for making sure your posts aren't mostly ads traces back to what we discussed at the beginning of this section.

Facebook breaks down the barrier between buyer and seller.

People are already used to being bombarded with ads on the radio and on television. But those advertisements are a one way street - clients don't get to interact, ask questions, or get engaged.

Ads are well and good, but they will be much more effective if your target audience is already interacting with you.

People want to see funny memes.

They want to see exciting pictures.

They want to read little anecdotes and clever sayings that they can post on their own profiles.

If the majority of your content is geared towards making your customers feel good, they will be way more receptive to your advertisements.

Scheduled Posting

If you don't have the budget to hire a social media manager, you might be thinking: "How am I ever going to find time to post on Facebook every day?"

Fortunately for you, Facebook makes it easy to schedule your posts in advance. This way, you can create one big batch of content and choose when you want it posted. Then, just sit back and let your content take care of itself.

Paid Vs. Organic Content

Facebook allows you to post both organic content and paid content. Both of them have their benefits.

Organic content is:

- Free to post

- Likely to reach your most loyal fans

- Never loses you money

Paid content is:

- Not free to post

- Reaches people who don't follow you yet

- Can generate significant ROI

I suggest you start with organic content. Once you have a good idea of what type of content your followers like to engage with, then you can start spending small amounts of money on your advertising budget. Remember, don't go all in at first. Spend as little as you can while you collect data. When you know what a global audience is likely to respond to, then you can consider boosting your advertising budget.

Choosing Your Audience

Facebook users voluntarily share a ton of information.

In turn, Facebook offers an audience tool that gives you access to 1000's of different data points to laser focus on exactly what your audience likes and the type of content they engage with.

Targeting too broad an audience is the biggest mistake I tend to see here.

Did you know that there are over **two and a half billion** active Facebook profiles in the world?

Chances are, they aren't all interested in what you are selling.

Narrow it down as much as possible. Your choices for parameters include age, gender, and location.

The most effective parameter, however, is interests.

If you are selling virtual mandolin lessons, do the obvious thing by targeting people who list mandolin as one of their interests. But go one step further. Target people who are interested in famous mandolin players, for example. The more specific you get, the better.

Remember, targeting is a paid service. To make it worthwhile, you need to be getting a good ROI. Narrowing down your niche as much as possible is the best way to do this.

Other Social Media Platforms

Instagram

Instagram is particularly useful for brands that rely heavily on visual content. Facebook's Ad Manager makes it very easy to connect your Facebook and Instagram accounts, which makes much of the techniques you will use on these platforms intertwined.

However, I would like to briefly discuss one element that is unique to Instagram.

Influencers

Influencers are people who have built up massive followings, due in part to their good tastes in new products. You can leverage this popularity by hiring them to promote your product in their posts. While the expenses can certainly rack up, your potential for ROI is massive.

Here are some of the benefits of hiring an influencer:

- Immediate Social Proof

Influencers have often spent years building their audience. They are fully devoted to interacting with their audience and creating the content their followers want to see. Therefore, the audience trusts them. They have some credibility. For the right price, you can use this to your advantage.

- Extended Outreach

Influencers put your product in front of audiences who you might not be able to reach through targeted advertising.

- Mutually Beneficial Relationships

Once you start to build your audience, you can begin sharing the influencer's posts on your own page. This will help them increase their followers and give them more incentive to continue working with you.

Pinterest

With nearly half a billion active users, Pinterest is a terrific tool for driving traffic to your website.

An exclusively visual platform, Pinterest's primary purpose is to inspire users. For example, if someone is planning a wedding, they may search for images with the hashtag #wedding.

From there, they will see images of tuxedos, dresses, exotic wedding locations, etc.

They can then create a "board," which is a collection of images related to their search.

So, for example, if you were a wedding planner, you could actively post images of successful events you have played a role in. Someone looking to get married might come across your profile and decide to check out your website. Just like that, you've boosted your traffic.

Snapchat/TikTok

These two apps are based on video content. While they don't have the leveraging ability of the previous platforms, they can be helpful to certain brands.

These apps have a very young demographic. Most of their users are in their teens or early twenties. As such, they are less likely to respond to traditional advertising techniques.

For many businesses, being on these apps is not essential.

For many others, it can be crucial!

If you are an artist, performer, public speaker, or someone who is selling themselves as the product, I highly recommend you make an account.

As for the content itself? It is constantly changing. The only way to truly understand it is to dive right in.

Make yourself an account, follow a few people in your niche and start scrolling. You will start to see what type of content starts conversations, how trends work, and how to start building your community.

Just a quick warning: these apps can be very addictive. Make sure the time you spend on them is beneficial to you and your business. You don't want to lose valuable work time while you are stuck in the infinite scroll!

Last Thoughts On Social Media

When it comes to successful marketing on social media, the golden rule is this:

There is no substitute for doing.

Don't wait to get started. Don't worry about not immediately getting the results you want. Just start doing it.

Keep testing your methods.

Keep improving.

Keep watching your conversions rise.

Additional Communication Strategies

Chatbots

Let's face it – the days of business being conducted from 9- 5 are probably gone for good. These days, people expect to be able to contact you at just about any hour of the day.

Does that mean you need to be in front of your computer at 3 AM to answer your clients' questions?

Of course not!

With chatbot technology, you can have a personalized conversation with your potential client at any hour of the day, even if you yourself are fast asleep.

Why Utilize Chatbots?

Customers want quick answers to their questions. If you can provide them with all the information they need right away, your CRO is sure to go up. Even if your page is well designed, some people just don't want to take the time to navigate through your FAQ page looking for what they want. With a chatbot, you can get them what they need right away.

Customers who engage with the chatbot are anywhere from 4-6 times more likely to convert. That's a huge difference!

Think of the chatbot as your digital sales representative. It is programmed to share your personality and values, and it's only job is to give clients what they want.

A quick Google search will reveal the many options you have for Chatbot technology. Every reputable service has its strengths, so research as much as you can before making an educated decision.

If you need some help setting up your chatbot technology, don't hesitate to contact our team at CROProfits.com/Call

Chatbot Best Practices

– Get Personal

This entire chapter is about strengthening your personal connection to your customers, and a chatbot is a great way to start. Business can be so impersonal these days, it is hard for customers to feel much of a connection at all to a company they haven't done business with yet.

When you set up your chatbot, you will be able to insert a custom greeting.
An unimaginative brand's greeting might just say 'Hello, how can I help you today?'

A brand looking to make a personal connection might say 'Thanks for checking out our gardening tools! How can we help improve your gardening experience?'

Right away, your customer will feel just a little more comfortable. And if they have a question about a specific pair of shears, now they have the perfect opportunity to ask.

– Let Your Client Get Comfortable Before Chatting

Like most online marketing professionals, I advise you to place your chatbot in a corner where it is noticeable, but doesn't dominate the page. There is a lot of debate about when your automated chat should begin. Some pages have the chat begin immediately.

From my research, I've found that clients find this technique a little too aggressive. I prefer to split test the conversation starter to trigger anywhere from 15-60 seconds into a session. This way, the customer has already shown enough interest to stay on the page, but hasn't had the time to find the answers they need just yet.

– Incorporate Chatbots Into Your Social Media Presence

You can also set up a chatbot to auto respond to messages sent to your Facebook page. This is helpful because people are already very used to Facebook's interface, so they are already coming from a position of trust.

- Make Your Responses Informative

Your clients may ask the chatbot a question such as "Are you accepting new clients?"

You could simply program the bot to respond 'Yes.'

Or, you could program it to say "Yes, I currently have openings Wednesday morning and Friday afternoon! Would you like to book an appointment?"

Just like in a real life conversation, this helps keep the lines of communication alive. It gives the client a reason to continue conversing. Ideally, you could link them directly to a page where they have the ability to make a booking.

Just like that, your chatbot has gotten you a new client!

- Have Your Chatbot Increase AOV

You can program your chatbot to make suggestions based on your visitor's activity. After they add an item to their cart, you can politely ask them if they would like to add a similar item. This is the equivalent of a salesperson saying 'Those shoes look great, we're running a sale on these socks that happen to match perfectly!'

- Test Everything

Try out different greetings, different timing, different names for your bot, different responses. Ideally, you want to create an experience that closely mimics a natural conversation. Don't worry if you don't get it right the first time! Just keep on testing until you start to see the results you want.

Live Chat

For regular working hours, you have the option of setting up an actual live chat. This is an even more effective method of answering your clients' questions and keeping them engaged with your content.

The pros of live chat are obvious – clients get the personalized service they need right away. On the flip side, you have to either make yourself available to do it, or hire a live agent to represent you. But if you do have the time and resources to establish a live chat, it's going to work wonders for your CRO results.

To gain the most benefit from this, have all customer facing departments available to assist the customer for whatever needs they have.

Live Chat Best Practices

Make It Clear That You Aren't A Bot

As we've established, chatbots can be very effective. But there is no substitute for real, human to human interaction. If asked a question, respond with as much detail as you can. Avoid one word answers. Instead, try to answer with a question to keep the conversation active.

Answer Right Away

Leaving your client's message unreturned is the digital equivalent of making them wait on hold. And there's nothing people hate more than being on hold. They could have just sent you an email if they had time to wait for a response. If you say you're online, you have to actually be available. This leads me to my next point.

Set Reasonable Hours

If you don't have the resources to hire a full time live agent, don't feel that you need to make yourself available 24/7. This is partially for your own well being as it will help you avoid unnecessary costs. It will also avoid irritating your customers, who will be unlikely to return if their messages are ignored.

email Marketing

While email marketing has been discussed elsewhere in this book, here, we will talk about it specifically in regards to the idea of building omnipresence with your customers.

With the possible exception of Facebook, Twitter, and Instagram, there are few platforms that people visit *every day*. That means you need to maintain a presence with your clients outside of your website. An ideal place to start is their inbox - one of the few things they do check every single day.

email Essentials

Be Relentless With Quality Control

I honestly can't tell you how many email lists I am on. I like to monitor the way people are handling their email lists and see if I can use that information to help my own communications.

One thing I have learned is that there is a *huge* disparity in quality between certain emails. There are some prominent writers and marketers whose emails I can't wait to open. I look forward to them all week, then sit down with a coffee and read every word. Sometimes they are sharing relatable work stories, other times they are relaying thoughtful advice on topics that don't even have to do with business. But no matter what the content is, I know that my time is being *valued*.

I'm a huge believer in quality over quantity here. If you

have the capabilities to turn out five productive emails a week, more power to you. But I believe it is much more effective to craft one thoughtful, helpful, and entertaining email every two weeks.

Offer Great Material For Free

In this era of endless information, it can be very difficult to stand out, even if you are accommodating a relatively small niche. You may promise that your email list contains the best beginner karate advice available. You may even be right!

But no one is going to take your word for it.

You need to prove it.

Write articles and blog posts on your site that prove your karate expertise.

Find your *slant* - the thing that makes you different from all the other gurus out there. Maybe it is your background, maybe it is your sense of humor. Whatever it is, once people are hooked on your free material, they will be a thousand times more willing to offer you their email address in return for more.

Consider Cross Promoting With A Guest Post

Online marketing guru Ramit Sethi claims that guest posting played a huge role in building his massive email list. It is a strategy that he continues to use to this day. He claims a recent guest post to Tim Ferriss' blog got him a substantial number of new followers.

Maybe you don't have any friends with massive followings yet. But do you know a few people in your niche who might consider hosting a guest post you've written (with a promise to return the favor of course)?

Write a particularly high quality post, and have your colleague post it on their blog. Include a clear Call To Action at the bottom, letting your new readers know where they can follow you and how they can sign up to your email list.

Cater To Your Most Devoted Readers

Even the largest email lists started out with a single subscriber. If you only have one follower right now, cater your material directly to them. Same thing if you have fifty followers. Out of all the people on earth, these fifty people have chosen to follow you. Don't worry about the billions who didn't. Focus on these devoted readers. If you churn out quality material at a consistent rate, more readers will come.

How To Craft An Effective email

Now that we have established some strategies for building your audience and discussed some philosophies to adhere to, let's get into the email itself.

In many ways, an email can be thought of as a mini sales funnel. Just like with your website, your first step is capturing your reader's attention.

Subject Line

Your subject line serves the same purpose as the headline of a page on your site - to make someone intrigued enough to want more.

There are, however, a few key differences.

Unlike with a page headline, your reader already knows who you are. So you do not have to introduce yourself.

Also, you will be crafting new headlines regularly, which gives you the ability to be significantly more creative.

Make it crystal clear what the email is about. Avoid subject lines like "Want to hear about our biggest sale ever?"

Instead, try "50% Off All Scarves For 48 Hours Only!"

If you are running a lifestyle brand based out of Chicago, don't write "Five Things To Do In The City."

Instead, how about "Five Northside Bars I Fell In Love With."

The key is to offer exactly the right amount of detail using as few words as possible.

Be Enthusiastic

Remember how I mentioned the emails I can't wait to read? Part of the reason for that is the enthusiasm they convey. The writer's positivity gets my blood flowing and makes me crave more.

Imagine your reader is having a relatively boring day at work. They're browsing their email during a lunch break, and they see your email. What will make their eyes light up with excitement? Consider this, and write accordingly.

Use Short Sentences

Short sentences are great. They keep you interested. They tell you what you need to know. They are easy to understand. Sure, there is a time and place where expanded, multi-part sentences will be beneficial to both you and your readers, but for now, share your story in as few words as possible. This will make writing less intimidating for beginners, while still leaving room for growth as you improve.

Avoid Typos At All Cost

With tools like Grammarly available for free, it should be easy to avoid any typos, especially on a relatively short email. They imply a lack of professionalism, and will quickly lose you followers.

Keep The Message Short

Time is short and attention spans are shorter. Get right to the point, say what needs to be said, then move along!

End With A Call To Action

Every email should end with the opportunity for the reader to find more content. Whether it is a link to your blog, your store, or your social media accounts, never miss an opportunity to continue building your relationship with your clients.

Customer Loyalty Programs

Customer loyalty programs have been around since long before the dawn of the eCommerce era. For example, maybe you remember those punch cards, where if you order 10 sandwiches, you receive the 11th for free?

Nowadays, of course, everything is managed online. But the concept remains the same. Give your most loyal customers a good reason to come back, and they will do so. You get more business, and they get free stuff, exclusive material, or whatever you choose to provide.

Customer Loyalty Program Best Practices

Give Your Client What You Know They Want

Look to popular fast food chains for inspiration. For example, Chipotle uses a point system with members of their loyalty program. Every time a customer places an order, they are rewarded a certain amount of points. Those points can later be exchanged for rewards ranging from a free entree to an extra side. You like their food, they want your business, it's a win- win.

Personalized Exclusive Content

Let's say you are a personal trainer who maintains a blog full of free, valuable content. You might consider offering a paid VIP subscription. For paying customers, you could offer personalized nutrition plans or even one on one zoom training sessions. This will offer you a chance to get to know your customers on a first name basis, which is, of course, a great way of retaining their business.

Keep It Simple

Don't overcomplicate your rewards system. Explain it in plain English, make it easy to join, and enjoy the process of strengthening your business relationships.

Virtual Events

Virtual events have become a quintessential part of modern life. Over the past few years, most of us have gotten used to conducting at least some of our professional and social lives through platforms such as Zoom or Facebook Messenger. Doesn't it follow suit that we should consider using virtual events to foster a sense of community around our businesses?

The type of event you choose will vary greatly depending on your niche.

People working in the entertainment industry regularly host live tweeting sessions to engage with their community.

Entrepreneurs attend virtual networking events. These can range from formal meetings to digital happy hours, but the goal is always to build relationships with like minded people who may be beneficial to each other.

Virtual classes have become very popular as well. You can take a guitar lesson, practice yoga, or learn how to cook a new dish all without leaving the comfort of your home.

I've personally taken part in countless webinars, both as a host and a student. There's nothing more exciting to me than getting the inside scoop from someone at the top of their industry. When I was getting my start, I would sometimes fly halfway around the world for such an opportunity. Now, it is just a few clicks away.

Virtual events are more advanced than some of the other techniques we have discussed here. But once you have amassed a steady following, they can be an invaluable tool.

Ask yourself the following questions:

- ☐ Am I building personal relationships with clients?

- ☐ Am I communicating enough with active visitors to my page?

- ☐ Is my email strategy effective?

- ☐ How can I reward loyal customers?

- ☐ Am I ready to start hosting virtual events?

Chapter Nine:

Make Your Blog Content Sizzle With Sales

> "I made a decision to write for my readers, not to try to find more readers for my writing."
> - Seth Godin

In this chapter, you will learn:

- ✓ How Blogging Can Send Your Sales Soaring
- ✓ How To Capture and Keep Your Reader's Attention
- ✓ How To Build Trust By Speaking Your Customer's Language
- ✓ The Power Of Storytelling
- ✓ How Blogging Can Improve Your Search Rankings
- ✓ How To Get Started, Even If You've Never Written Before
- ✓ How To Go From Beginner To Professional

Once reserved for hobbyists and aspiring writers, blogs are now a ubiquitous part of the eCommerce landscape. From the smallest specialty shops to global operations, nearly every successful company is running a blog. Blogging regularly can help you:

- Convert More Sales
- Generate Leads
- Improve Search Rankings
- Demonstrate Expertise
- Advertise New Products
- Give Customers a Reason To Return

If you've never written a blog before, you might feel a little intimidated. But don't worry, you don't need to be a trained writer to construct an effective blog post. In fact, I'd estimate that the vast majority of bloggers have no formal training whatsoever. Follow these simple guidelines, and your blog will be off the ground in no time.

Grab Readers' Attention Right Away With An Urgent Headline

"If Your Car Is Doing This, You Could Be At Risk Of Engine Failure"

"It's Time To Take Control Of Your Fitness"

"The Superfood You Haven't Heard About Yet"

Each one of these headlines creates a sense of urgency. If I have even a passing interest in cars, I'm going to want to know what to do to prevent engine failure. If your blog successfully educates me, I'm going to come back every time I'm having car trouble.

It is important to be honest here! Avoid unreasonable headlines and impossible promises. Headlines like these encourage people to not take you seriously:

"Your Car Could Explode At Any Minute!"

"How To Get The Perfect Body In Seven Days."

"The Superfood Guaranteed To Regrow Your Hair"

You get the idea. Be urgent, but be honest.

Creating a great headline is not often as easy as it looks. You have to convey exactly what you are talking about, who you are talking to, and why it is important to listen within ten words or less. Here are a few more key pointers when crafting your headline:

– Stick To The Big Picture

Of course you have plenty of information to share. And why wouldn't you? You are an expert in this field! But your headline is not the place to share that information. Just say exactly what you are talking about, and leave it at that.

– Keywords

Get to your keywords as fast as possible. The sooner in the headline you use them, the better search results you will get.

A good example looks like this:

"Lose Ten Pounds In Two Months"

A bad example looks like this:

"In Only Two Months, You Could Lose Ten Pounds"

In the first example, we see the important part of our topic right away. In the second example, we don't get to the point until the very end of the headline. It may seem like a small difference, but that can be the difference between capturing your reader's attention right away and losing them for good.

Speak Your Customer's Language

"Do you know what a mandible is? Your dentist does. So if you're writing for dentists, use the word 'mandible.' If not, use the word 'jaw.'" - Gary Provost

Your blog is an opportunity to show that you know what you're talking about. So use their lingo. Don't be afraid to get technical. This is where you get to really hone in the intricacies of your field. Think

117

back to Sweetwater and how they used guitar-specific language to excite their customers. It may help to picture this as a casual conversation between two people with a shared interest.

Answer Your Client's Specific Question

This is a great way to boost your search rankings. Many Google searches start with phrases like 'How do I...' or "What do I need to...". Keep that question in your mind as you write your blog.

When your post is finished, ask yourself: *Have I answered the reader's question?*

Again, this is a great opportunity to get specific. If you are marketing to sailboat enthusiasts, you don't need to share everything you know about sailboats in a single post. Just pick a common question and answer it clearly, efficiently, and enthusiastically. Bad examples would be:

> *"Everything You Have Ever Wanted To Know About Sailboats"*

> *"What I Have Learned From Sailing"*

> *"Problems With Your Sailboat? This Could Be The Reason"*

More Effective examples would like like this:

> *"Purchasing Your First Sailboat On A Budget"*

> *"Great Sailing Destinations For This Winter"*

> *"Sailboat Engine Troubleshooting For Beginners"*

Tell A Story

Who doesn't love a good story? Stories can help illustrate your point. They give your writing a personal touch. Remember, you are not writing a technical manual here. You are both educating your reader and building a relationship with them. Make them feel seen. Show them that you have been in their shoes – you have made the progress that they would like to make, and you are enthusiastic about helping them achieve their goals.

Let's say for example that you are writing a blog for competitive chili cooks. (It's a very real thing!)

Which of these examples of an opening paragraph is more interesting?

- Option 1

"As the winner of ten local chili cook-offs, I have learned a lot. The secret is to make sure beef is just browned enough before you put it into the pot. After that, you'll want to get the perfect blend of spices. Many beginners add too much salt, so be sure not to do that."

- Option 2

"When I entered my first chili cook-off at forty years old, I'll admit, I was a little intimidated. All the other chefs were so talented. I wondered how they got their beef so perfectly tender and what mixture of spices they were using. Now, several years later, I've won ten local chili competitions, and I'm aiming at number eleven this summer. I'm going to show you the exact technique I now use to brown my beef, and, as a bonus, I'll show you my general rule of thumb for getting a distinctive blend of spices. Hint: There's no such thing as too much cumin."

I can't tell you which of these writers is a better chef. But I can certainly tell you which one I would rather discuss chili with. Option 1 comes off as bland and boastful. He only offers generic advice and doesn't answer a single specific question. I might as well be reading the back of a can of chili.

Option 2, on the other hand, immediately comes off as personable and relatable. He starts by recognizing how difficult this recipe is to perfect. Then he assures me that I can do it too. Finally, he promises in depth solutions to two common questions. I'm hooked, and ready to read more.

You may ask yourself, why do I have to do this at all? Why can't I just jump right in with the recipe? The answer has to do with Google's SEO algorithm.

Google has a way of inherently filtering out what they consider to be 'Low Quality Content.' They consider very short posts to be low quality, and therefore,

worthy of lower placement in their search rankings.

Case Studies

Once Upon A Chef

To further demonstrate this concept, I Googled 'How To Cook A Steak.' The top result is from the blog OnceUponAChef.com And no surprise, it follows all the rules we have laid out here. Let's break it down to see why, on such a popular topic, Google considers this blog to be the most beneficial.

Headline

'How To Cook Steak On The Stove Top'

Not rocket science, but incredibly effective. The word 'Steak' shows up early. It includes a specific aspect – the 'stove top.' And it captures my attention using only eight syllables.

Sub- Header

'Pan searing is the best way to cook a steak, and it's also the easiest!'

If I've just Googled 'How To Cook A Steak,' that probably means that I'm no chef myself. So the words 'best' and 'easiest' immediately jump out at me. That's good enough for me to continue reading the article.

Opening Paragraphs

'I love the kind of dinner that you can cook without a recipe. The truth is, good cooking is more about technique than recipes and the best dishes are often the simplest to prepare. A properly cooked steak is case in point. With just a few ingredients and a single pan, you can cook a steak that's as delicious as one you'd order in a high-end steakhouse.

'The key is knowing how to pan-sear. Pan-searing is a classic technique in which the surface of the food is cooked undisturbed in a very hot pan until a crisp, golden-brown, flavorful crust forms. It's the key to building flavor and texture in a dish. It also prevents sticking and gives your food a restaurant-quality look. Pan-searing is the absolute best way to cook a steak (salmon, too), and it also happens to be the easiest.

The opening sentence reaffirms the writer's passion for cooking. As we have stated, enthusiasm is incredibly important. She then goes on to reassure me that I can make a great steak if I try out the technique she is about to show me. She lets me know that it is going to be easy by mentioning that I only need a few ingredients and a single pan.

In the second paragraph, she gets into the specifics of 'Pan-searing,' which again, as an amateur chef, I'm presumably not too familiar with. She even lets me know that this technique can also be helpful with other popular dishes.

(Notice that she linked to another article on her blog? We'll get into that topic next.)

In the rest of the post, she confidently explains how to make this recipe. It is detailed, in-depth, and clearly written with the beginner in mind. It is easy to see why this post performs so well on Google.

Internal Linking

SEO loves pages that keep people engaged and connect them with other relevant pages. You know how YouTube is constantly recommending similar videos to the one you just watched? The same concept applies here. By linking to other blog posts or product pages within your site, you create a miniature collection of content. This ensures Google that you are actively posting quality material that people want to see.

Here are some best practices for internal linking:

- Put at least one link at the top of your page

Seeing that link right away lets your reader know that your blog is to be taken seriously. And since most people make a decision about whether to continue reading within a matter of seconds, that first impression is a great start.

- Link to content that is directly relevant

In the previous example, an article about steak linked to an article about salmon. If I'm interested in one, I might be interested in the other. Don't include links just for the sake of it - make sure they include valuable content. The almighty SEO knows the difference.

Generating New Ideas And Overcoming Writer's Block

Every writer on the planet has experienced writer's block at some point (and yes, you are a writer now). Fortunately, there are plenty of effective methods of overcoming what writers dramatically refer to as 'the tyranny of the blank page.'

Read

You can't be a good writer if you aren't a good reader. If you feel like you're running on empty, maybe it is time to take a break and refresh your mind with some new ideas. Reading just about anything will help you generate new ideas. It can be a business blog, a novel, even just a well written email. When you sit back down to type, you'll be almost guaranteed to have some new ideas to work with.

Copy

Yes, literally, copy.

In his genre defining book '100 Ways To Improve Your Writing,' Gary Provost wrote:

"Take a few words from something you enjoyed reading...and copy them word for word...In time you will feel like an insider, and you will say, "'I know why he chose this word; I know why he wrote two short sentences instead of one long one.'"

Gary's writing techniques made him a household name in the business community, so it's probably worth giving it a shot! Take a look at the blog of any business you enjoy. You could also select one from a business that we have analyzed. Pick a paragraph and manually copy it word for word. As you do so, consider every aspect of what you are writing.

How was the topic introduced?

Are the sentences long or short?

Are they making statements or asking questions?

Each little detail you pick up from a successful blog will help you improve your own writing.

Keep A Running List Of Ideas

Trust me, you won't be the first person to have a brilliant idea while they are sitting in traffic with no access to a computer. When inspiration strikes, take note! That way you can always go back to your idea later. Write it down in a notebook or speak into your smart phone's voice recorder. Just don't let that great idea go to waste!

Case Study

One of the great things about blogging, and eCommerce in general, is the sense of community. In the blogging world, people can behave the same way they would in real life - as equals. There is no barrier between writer and reader. If you agree with something you read in a blog, you can share it on your own page - or you can reach out directly to the author to thank them for the knowledge they've imparted. If you disagree, you have an open forum to make your counterargument.

In a world where connections mean everything, blogs are one of the best tools you have at your disposal.

Just a few positive responses can give you the encouragement you need to keep going.

A negative response might give you a reason to revalue your position and try to do better next time.

Above all, blogs are a place for ideas.

And ideas are the first step in any process. Apple, Microsoft, and Tesla all started as simple ideas.

The venture that is going to change your life will start with an idea as well.

Here's the thing about ideas though: They rarely happen in a vacuum.

The famous musician and international artist David Byrne coined the phrase - scenius - a mixture of the words scene and genius. He believed that people did their greatest work when they were immersed in a community of like minded individuals who were united by a pursuit of similar goals.

Once you get involved in the blogging community, you have instant access to

any 'scene' at the tip of your fingers. For this next example, I'd like to share with you a blog that has been a source of constant inspiration for me - The Moz.

The Moz Blog

Moz is not just the work of one individual. It is a constantly changing website created by a group of like minded individuals that are passionate about SEO. As such, I know that every time I visit the blog, I'm going to find something that is valuable to me.

I may not agree with everything they post, but I know that at the very least, I will be challenged. At best, I might find an idea that will spark my next business pursuit.

In this case study, we are going to closely look at both the layout, and the philosophies that make this blog so successful.

Let's start at Moz.com/blog

The first thing I notice is

how visually appealing this page is. It strikes a perfect balance between minimalist design and eye popping imagery. Above the fold, I can see links to two recent articles, both written by experts in SEO.

I'm going to check out the most recent post, which as of today, is a post titled:

"The Top Tech SEO Strategies for 2022 and Beyond" by Crystal Carter

(Note: By the time you read this, there will of course be a new top post)

This is a great title that immediately draws me in. They know that this blog is frequented by people like myself, who are always trying to stay at the forefront of the SEO world. Therefore, the word beyond immediately catches my eye.

Underneath, we can see two tags, or subcategories: Technical SEO and Advanced SEO. Again, perfect for their target audience.

Below that, we see a one paragraph excerpt from the post. This serves two purposes:

- To excite the reader

- To inform them about what specific topics the post will be covering

And then, finally, we have a pleasant blue button labeled 'Read this post.'

Let's click on that and see what this post has to offer!

On the next page, I'm greeted by the same imagery that I saw in the preview - great for creating consistency. There are plenty of headlines and subheadlines- great for organizational purposes. And I also see plenty of visual content. All these factors combine to make me feel welcome before I've read a word.

Now let's check out the actual content.

Opening Paragraph

The post begins:

"Last year was an incredible year for Core Updates."

The author has done a terrific job of portraying her enthusiasm in the first sentence. If the writer is enthusiastic, it encourages a similar feeling for the reader.

Early in your post, either in the headline or opening paragraph, it is always good to use words like **incredible** or **amazing**. Later on, switch to more everyday words like **good**, or **great**.

The rest of the opening paragraph is full of words that let me see exactly what I am going to read about. This puts me in the mindset I need to be in to get the most out of what I am about to read.

The Bulk Of The Article

Scrolling down to the bulk of the article, I see another headline and sub-headline:

Multimedia First

Why should you consider a multimedia-first SEO strategy?

The title tells me exactly which topic I'm going to write about.

Did you notice that the author's sub-headline is written in the form of a question? This is a great writing technique, especially if your audience is prone to critical thinking.

Asking them a question automatically sends their brain into curiosity mode. They have every reason to continue reading.

Then I get into the real bulk of the post. The first sentence of this paragraph reads:

"MUM is the latest in Google's suite of super- powerful algorithms..."

Now I won't get into too much detail here, but this speaks directly to an SEO obsessive like me. The author has immediately established herself as a genuine *expert* in her topic. I'd be crazy not to keep reading.

> Note: When you're ready for super advanced SEO techniques, I highly recommend you look this post up.

As I continue scrolling down, I find a wealth of information. There are charts, graphs, and diagrams. There are links to relevant material. There are detailed instructions on how to tap into Google's latest tools to get the best possible SEO results.

By the time I get to the end of the article, I feel as if I've just sat through a college-level lecture. I can't wait to start implementing the author's ideas. And of course, I'm going to follow the author and share her ideas with my friends and colleagues.

This is blogging at its best.

I've been provided with tremendous value, the author has been given valuable exposure, and the entire online business community has been made just a little bit stronger.

As your blog continues to grow, I highly suggest you think of yourself as a part of a community. Maybe you haven't found your people yet, but I assure you, they are out there. And they want to hear from you.

Don't wait until you think you are 'ready.'

Start writing today and become a part of something important.

Conclusion

Yes, blogging leads to a major increase in sales and leads to much higher search results. But above all, it is fun! This should be one of the most enjoyable parts of running your business. So don't take it too seriously. Follow the guidelines I've laid out for you in this chapter and start sharing your thoughts with the world. When thinking about your blog, ask yourself the following questions:

☐ Have I captured my reader's attention with catchy headlines?

☐ Do my readers have a good reason to stick around?

☐ Is my blog visually appealing?

☐ Am I using the right keywords?

☐ Am I conveying enough enthusiasm?

☐ What communities would I like to be a part of?

_____

☐ How can I use my blog to improve my readers' lives?

_____

Chapter Ten:
With CRO, Data Is King

"No great marketing decisions have ever been made on qualitative data."
— John Sculley.

In this chapter you will learn:

- ✓ How to identify your core demographic

- ✓ The best sources of beneficial data

- ✓ How to maximize your decision making abilities

- ✓ How data can help turn your vision into a reality

Getting visitors to your page isn't all that hard.

Getting them to spend their money, on the other hand, is extremely challenging.

If there is one recurring theme that we need to emphasize, it's that 'Data Is King.'

Above all, CRO is about how to gather analytical data and make informed decisions to further grow your conversions.

Here are some data strategies that should always be at the forefront of your mind as you start to dive deeper into the numbers of your business.

Analyze Your Audience

There is a common saying in sales - "Find out what keeps your clients awake at night." Let's think about what that means. Sales is not just about giving people what they want. It's about fixing their problems and improving their lives. We've discussed this a lot, and for good reason. You can't overstate the importance of understanding your audience. Let's discuss some key data points you should learn about your audience - some of them are simple and easy to quantify - others are more existential. All of them will help you turn visitors into customers.

- Age

A twenty year old on the internet behaves very differently than a seventy year old. But they are both willing to spend, if you market correctly. Younger people tend to be averse to traditional sales methods. They are more interested in organic content that reveals the personality behind the brand. They are likely hanging out on TikTok and Snapchat. Older audiences, on the other hand, tend to congregate more on Facebook. They're more likely to click on traditional advertisements. Consider your target demographic's age, and adapt your strategy accordingly.

- Device

Today, businesses need to be everywhere. As we have mentioned elsewhere, a majority of shoppers report having made a purchase from their phone in the last six months. Closely analyze what devices your clients are using, and make sure you are catering directly to them.

- Profession/Income

If you're reading this, there's a good chance that you are an ambitious entrepreneur. You're passionate about running an eCommerce operation, so you're happy to spend your money on CRO research. That's why I've tailored this book exactly to people like you. Someone who happily works a regular job, on the other hand, isn't going to be spending their money on this type of thing. So what are they spending their money on? Your job is to find this data from market research. If you're selling luxury goods and experiences, there's no reason to market your product to individuals with low incomes. If you're selling extremely affordable items that rely on bulk sales to make a profit, you should be marketing to a very broad audience.

Lessons Learned From Price Analysis

I'd like to tell you a couple of stories about some interesting things I've learned from analyzing price data. I was once hired to analyze a local landscaping company. They had been experiencing a major lull in their sales, and they needed answers. So I came in and started testing right away. What I found was that people in this neighborhood simply weren't interested in spending a lot of money on landscaping. We ran multiple ads with different headlines. The most effective by far was 'The Most Affordable Landscaping In Town.' Once we started marketing the company as a discount operation, sales immediately went up.

Next up - a dog daycare company that I worked with. We had the exact opposite experience! By actually raising their prices, we sent the message that this was a high end experience. Everyone loves their dogs, and they are more than happy to spend more if they think it means a better experience. Again, we came to this conclusion through a lot of trial and error. But once we were certain about our strategy, we implemented it to perfection.

Best Sources To Collect Data

- Shopify Analytics

A basic Shopify account includes a complex data analysis system that will tell you everything you need to know about your clients' behavior *while they are visiting the page*. They also provide plenty of free educational materials that will show beginners how to understand and analyze the aforementioned data.

- Facebook Analytics

Just like Shopify, Facebook has become a key player in eCommerce by making their platform easily accessible to anyone. You can see data specific to everything you post, making your social media activity one of the easiest things to optimize.

- Customer Surveys

If you want more personalized feedback, consider asking customers to take a survey. Many people are happy to share their thoughts about their experiences. You can also further incentivize them by offering discounts on future purchases, or any other benefit you think they would enjoy.

- Cookie/Pixel Tracking

Advanced, but very useful! We've covered this topic extensively elsewhere in the book.

The Changing World Of Data Analysis

Here is a phrase you will hear commonly, not just in this book, but in everyday life:

"We are more connected than ever before."

From a marketing point of view, here is what that statement really means:

"We are sharing more data than ever before."

An entire generation has grown up regularly sharing pictures of their meals before eating them. They regularly post their exact geographical location, tagging themselves everywhere from the cafes where they have coffee to the beaches where they go to relax.

Marketers used to spend immeasurable time and energy trying to gain access to this detailed level of data.

Now? Potential customers happily and knowingly give it away for free.

And it isn't just young people anymore.

Just about every person you know leaves a constant trail of data – from the instant they get up in the morning to the moment they fall asleep at night.

Now that marketers have easy access to this data, you would think that business would be through the roof across industries.

But an alarming amount of new entrepreneurs barely even scratch the surface of what can be accomplished.

Here are a few key things you can do once you've gathered the appropriate amount of data:

– Anticipate Your Customer's Needs

The marketer's main job is to make your customer's life happier, easier, and more fulfilling, correct? Well, they are telling you exactly what they want. If your data shows that most of your demographic does their shopping on a mobile device, make sure that is the focus of your attention. If your data tells you that they are willing to subscribe to your content for $9.99 but not $19.99, change your prices accordingly.

– Stop Wasting Money

Let's face it, most of us don't start out with a huge advertising budget. If you're going to be spending money on paid content, you need to be certain that it is worth it. If you are running a few different ads and only seeing sporadic ROI, it is time to mix up your strategy.

Don't make the mistake of thinking you can casually

keep track of your data. IE "Hmm this ad seems to be doing better than the other one."

Keep detailed notes. Make spreadsheets. Leave nothing to the imagination. This way, you'll never waste another cent on an underperforming asset.

Don't have time for complex data analysis? Don't let that stop you! Visit CROProfits.com/call and hire us, the professionals, who know all the ins and outs of making profitable data driven decisions.

– Strong Data Instincts

Using data analytics doesn't just make your business more profitable, it makes it more human.

It can tell you when to trust the numbers and when you can follow your instincts.

For example, let's say you have a passion that you would like to turn into a profitable business. But you're worried that it is an unattainable goal. So you start doing a little research. You find out that there are already a handful of small businesses succeeding in your niche. And now you know: It is possible to succeed.

That is simple yes or no data in its purest form.

But let's say it isn't quite enough to reassure you just yet.

You start building your eCommerce store during your time off from your full time job. And you start to collect data on the free content you post to Facebook. Your photo content doesn't seem to get any responses at all. But your video content, on the other hand, is getting a lot of likes.

So you narrow it down further.

It turns out that video content in which you appear in the frame is more effective than your other options. So you start to focus your energy there. Now engagement is peaking. You decided you're ready for a bigger audience. You can confidently start advertising this specific form of video content, because it has been indisputably proven as effective.

Now you are being viewed across the country. Even if your CRO is still a humble 1%, you've dramatically increased your chances of conversions.

After a while, you have enough customers to switch your full time job to part time. Now, you have more time to focus on your passion.

And it's all thanks to data!

Conclusion

I guarantee you this: The amount of data you have at your fingertips right now is all you need to start multiplying your conversions. It is simply a matter of knowing how to use it. Ask yourself these questions:

☐ How could I use data to gain a better understanding of my demographic?

_____

☐ What specific attributes can I learn about my customers?

_____

☐ Where is my data coming from?

_____

- ☐ Do I have enough data to consistently make well-informed decisions?

- ☐ If not, how do I gather more data?

- ☐ How can proper data analysis make my business more profitable and more fulfilling?

Chapter Eleven:

Important Stats For Online Sales Growth

"When you undervalue what you do, the world will undervalue who you are."
- Oprah Winfrey

In this chapter you will learn:

- ✓ A Series Of Important Statistics That Put The Value Of CRO In Context

- ✓ How To Implement Statistics Into Your Process

In a perfect world, 100% of your visitors would become clients.

Even 25% would be fantastic!

But the truth is, even the most successful eCommerce operations only convert about 5% of their visitors.

I don't tell you this to discourage you, of course. In fact, this should be reassuring. Just getting from 1% to 5% is enough to put you into the upper echelon of the sales world.

Here are some key statistics you should keep in mind:

- **The average online retail outlet has a conversion rate of about 3%**

- **The average Shopify store has a conversion rate of about 1.5%.**

I theorize that this is due to many amateur entrepreneurs not taking the time to properly optimize their operation with CRO.

- **About 97% of visitors never make it past a store's landing page**

Remember all the strategies we've discussed for designing landing pages? This statistic should reaffirm how important this is.

- **Only 18% of marketers utilize A/B Testing**

Can you believe that? Think of how much you'll set yourself apart from the crowd if you use these techniques.

- **93% of sales start with an online search.**

This is why we've placed so much emphasis on SEO (Search Engine Optimization).
If you're not showing up in organic searches, you're not making sales. Fortunately, this is one of the most easily improved aspects of your page.

- **Business To Business operations have an average conversion rate of nearly 10%**

(Note: If you're running a B2B, this is great news!)

- **Email campaigns can boost conversions by up to 4%**

Are you communicating with potential customers constantly? If not, now is the time to start!

- **The average Facebook ad converts at over 9%**

The social media world may have changed a lot over the years, but when it comes to online marketing, Facebook is still king. There is no better platform for effectively targeting and selling to your niche market.

- **Conversion rates vary wildly by industry**

Financial and legal companies tend to be the top performers, often converting at rates of over 6%.

- **80% of users are more likely to make a purchase if the landing page conveys trust**

Trust is everything - making a good first impression is key to the entire sales funnel, so test away and make sure your landing page is in top form.

Ask yourself the following questions:

☐ How do these statistics relate to my operation?

☐ What reasonable goals can I set to improve my own statistical performance?

Chapter Twelve:

User Testing = Goldmine

"The best investment is in the tools of one's own trade."
– Benjamin Franklin

In this chapter, you will learn:

- ✓ What UX means

- ✓ How To Optimize UX

- ✓ How Heat Maps Work

- ✓ How Live User Testing Works

- ✓ What You Can Learn From User Testing

Now, we're going to cover the popular topic of User Experience, commonly shortened to UX.

And more importantly, we will discuss all the ways you can test your UX to achieve your highest possible conversion rate.

Some topics will be specific, others will be more philosophical.

As always, the right mixture of art and science is a recipe for CRO success.

The noted data architect Peter Morville established six core attributes to creating a successful UX. A web page needs to be useful, usable, desirable, findable, accessible, and credible. Let's get into detail about every one of these elements.

– Useful

This attribute can be hard to define and requires a little bit of outside the box thinking. What is useless to one person can be very useful to another. Some products are so useful that they are considered essential ie) healthcare, shelter, food, etc. Other products may not serve a tangible need, but they still have an important purpose. These products might make people feel better about themselves, make their apartment feel more like a home, or maybe they're just plain fun.

If the service you are offering is essential, design your UX accordingly. Remind people why they need what you're selling. Emphasize what makes you stand out from the competition. If you're selling something that isn't essential, remind your customer why this product is useful to them.

- Usable

This one is a biggie. It is also one of the elements we will be testing the most. An intuitive layout is absolutely essential to boosting your conversion rate. All it takes is a single misplaced button, broken link, or questionable design choice to lose a customer. Much more on this to come.

- Desirable

Great brands make us feel something right away. When we see McDonalds' yellow arches, we get hungry. Apple Computer's fruit design makes us feel ambitious. Your favorite sports team's logo gets you excited. Your logo - and the rest of your design choices - should do something similar. If you are the logo designer yourself, it can be hard to separate yourself from the results. Don't just go with your favorite imagery - test out your options. Create multiple designs and ask your friends, family, and coworkers which they like best. Better yet, integrate these designs and split test them. After a few hundred people have viewed them, it will be very clear to you which design you should be using.

- Findable

People need to be able to find your business. In the old days, this might have meant putting up a giant billboard at a busy intersection. Nowadays, it's much more affordable and manageable. Find out where your customers spend their time online, and place your ads there. Use the tactics we have discussed to boost your SEO. Test out different headlines, articles, social media posts, etc to find the best one. Then, share it as much as you possibly can.

– Accessible

79% of people report having made a purchase from their smartphone in the last six months. So bear in mind that is no longer enough to just have a good desktop webpage. This leaves too much money on the table. Your page needs to be formatted for mobile devices, and just as easy to use. Certain webpage design functions will do this automatically. Other times, if you don't have an internal team to handle this, it would then be a great idea to hire a freelance designer to help you.

– Credible

We've discussed this

extensively elsewhere, but it bears repeating. Make it indisputable to your clients that your page is safe. If you don't, be sure that they will take their money elsewhere.

Methods Of Testing

So now you've taken the time to create what you believe to be the best possible user experience. But, how do you know if it is really working? In this section, we will discuss two very specific ways of testing your UX. Remember, the results might be humbling, but don't shy away from them. Most amateur marketers never take this step. That's what makes them stay amateurs. By wholeheartedly embracing this process, you'll be ready to go pro in no time.

Heat Mapping

Note: The following section discusses a very technical topic. If you know how to code or are an advanced web designer, you will find many great methods. If not, you may want to consider giving our team a shout at <u>CROProfits.com/call</u> as we'd be more than happy to help!

- What is a Heat Map?

A heat map is a tool that shows you exactly how users are behaving on your website, down to the littlest detail. You can see what they do with their mouses, which sections they stop to read, what they're skipping, and where they're clicking. And best of all, it puts all that data into a visual form that anyone can understand.

There are three main types of heat maps.

- Click Maps

Simple maps that show which area of your page is getting the most clicks. Frequently clicked areas appear in red, while less frequently clicked areas appear in blue. In order for your sales funnel to function smoothly, users need to be clicking where you want them to. If they're not progressing further into your page, something is wrong. This tool can help you identify why. Maybe you have a call to action button placed in an unnatural location. Maybe your design is too cluttered and people can't decide where to click. A heat map gives you the data you need to fix whatever the problem may be.

- Move Maps

A move map focuses exclusively on your user's cursor. You can see if they are hovering in a certain area but not clicking. This can help to determine if your page is effectively holding your customers' attention. If their cursor is all over the place, something is wrong. There may be too much content or there may not be enough. Testing is the only way to find out.

– Scroll Maps

Scroll maps are particularly helpful for product listings. They simply show how far users are scrolling down your page. Ideally, they would be going down all the way to the bottom, but that's rarely the case. Use this tool to see how much of your users' attention you are holding, then determine which products you could add to help them descend further down. The further down they scroll, the more likely you are to make a sale.

There are many options for heat mapping software – some customer favorites include Hotjar, FigPii, and Mouseflow. Some tools are entirely free, some offer free trials, and some are paid. If you are going to undertake this step by yourself, I recommend you try out as many options as possible – get comfortable with the software and gather as much data as you can. If you find yourself overwhelmed, don't hesitate to reach out to a pro!

Heat Mapping Best Practices

Place Your Heat Maps In The Correct Places

While they are extremely useful, heat maps also require a lot of work. They are time consuming, expensive, and packed to the brim with data that directly correlates to your page's performance.

So don't overload yourself with information by putting a heat map on every single page of your website.

149

Instead, focus on the most important ones - the landing page and the checkout page. You could put one on a single product page, but don't feel the need to put them on every single one. Your customers probably behave similarly on any product page.

Set Specific Goals

Setting specific goals will help you streamline your process. For example, let's say that you are driving plenty of traffic to your landing page, but none of them are going any further into your sales funnel. A heat map placed solely on the landing page will help you determine why.

Make Sure The Data Isn't Skewed

If you are running a company, make sure that the company's IP address is blocked from your testing protocols. If your employees are frequently using the website, the data they enter will be irrelevant and taint your results.

While heat maps are great, they should not be your sole resource for finding data about your visitor's behavior. Make sure you involve the human element as well! This brings me to my next point.

Live User Testing

This method involves hiring ordinary people to test out your site. For example, you might give them a specific task and time how long it takes them to complete it.

A few services I recommend that offer this are:
UserTesting.com
TryMyUi.com

Unlike a heat map, which simply reports on user activity and turns it into data, these services let you watch how real people use your site.

Additionally, you have the option of providing them with surveys to share their experiences.

Or better yet, you can have them comment in real time.

Their feedback will prove to be invaluable.

Here's an example of how I might set up a live user test.

Let's say I run an athletic equipment store. I would envision a hypothetical situation in which a parent needs to buy a very specific piece of sports gear for their child. The child could be a baseball player, he loves Adidas, and he wears a size seven shoe. I would explain this task to them, and then monitor the actions. Now bear in mind, this tester may not be technically savvy, and furthermore may not know much about baseball.

This is a very realistic scenario that will really emphasize how ordinary people are behaving on my page. Ideally, I would view their screen remotely. This helps simulate a natural shopping experience. I would also give the tester a prepaid credit card or coupon code, so that they can complete the entire transaction just like in real life.

Next, we analyze their feedback.

Was it easy to get from the landing page to the baseball products page? Were they overwhelmed by the amount of Adidas we offered? Maybe we had one popular pair advertised as our 'Best Seller,' which made her select it. Hopefully, it was easy for the tester to find the right size.

In real life, if our user encountered any trouble along the way, they would likely just abandon the page.

They would shop at one of the countless other stores that sell baseball cleats and never give my store a second thought. The beauty of live testing is that we get to hear a customer's thought process at the exact moment their shopping experience becomes less than ideal.

Most likely, our live tester won't be speaking to us in technical terms. For example, they are not going to say: "You should have shown four items per row in your product grid instead of six." Instead, they might say something like "I felt overwhelmed."

Your job is to listen to their problem in generalized terms, then find a specific solution.

Here is another potential scenario you could put your live testers in:

Let's say that you are a nutritionist and chef who creates personalized diet plans for clients. Your pricing structure looks like this:

A- $125 for seven meals a week

B- $175 for fourteen meals a week

C- $200 for twenty- one meals a week

This is a common pricing structure. It is designed to emphasize that option C provides the best value. As a business owner, you are hoping that your customer chooses the package which results in the most purchases. But without split testing your pricing structure, you never truly know what your customers are willing to pay. This will result in you leaving a lot of money on the table.

So you hire a group of live testers. Ask them to spend five minutes browsing your site, then decide which package they would be most likely to choose.

Ideally, a majority would choose C.

But let's say they don't.

Ask them why they didn't choose C.

Most of them would probably respond "Package C seems a little too expensive for me."

Fair enough.

Next, you would invite in a new group of testers. Keep A and B the same, but try changing the price of the C package to $195.

Now, I am willing to bet many more testers selected C. Even though your price per order has gone down slightly, you will make up for it by fulfilling a higher number of orders.

Without testing, there is only guessing.

Live User Testing Best Practices

Have a Plan In Place

Of course, you want to improve your conversion rate. But, before you get started, it is important to know exactly what data you are trying to collect. Your testing sections should have tangible, measurable goals. Discuss them clearly with your team before beginning your session.

Don't "Lead" Your Customers

You are looking for a window into how your potential customers actually think. Don't interrupt their natural process by asking them leading questions, such as "Did you feel like our product descriptions were too long or too short?" Instead, ask something more general, such as "Tell me how you felt while browsing the product pages."

Have a Large Sample Size

Data is only relevant if you are drawing from a large, diverse pool of users. Some will be more tech savvy than others. Some will be prone to impatience or frustration. Make sure you aren't skewing your results by only testing your page with a handful of people.

Conclusion:

Never underestimate the wealth of information you can gain through user testing. You'll never have a better opportunity to see exactly what makes them tick. As you begin the ongoing process of user testing, ask yourself the following questions:

☐ Have I created an efficient user experience?

_____

☐ What can be improved about my UX?

_____

☐ What testing methods would be most effective for me?

_____

☐ How can I incorporate the feedback I've received?

_____

Chapter Thirteen:

Boost Your CRO Results With The Power Of Retargeting

"It's hard to find things that won't sell online."
– Jeff Bezos

In this chapter you will learn:

- ✓ How to approach retargeting ethically

- ✓ The fundamental aspects of retargeting

- ✓ How to set up a retargeting campaign using Google

- ✓ How to set up a retargeting campaign using Facebook

- ✓ What your retargeting campaign should include

- ✓ How retargeting can actually get you new leads

- ✓ The science behind why retargeting is so effective

If you've followed all the strategies shared up to this point, congratulations, you are now better off than most!

Now it's time to steam roll your competition.

In this chapter, we will discuss some of the advanced techniques that can truly put you in the upper echelon of eCommerce. While some of the technical lingo here may be intimidating,

I assure you, with some patience and persistence, you will come to understand everything you need to know about taking your business to the next level with the power of retargeting.

As always, if you'd like specialized guidance, I advise you to contact us directly at CROProfits.com/call

Foreword About Privacy And Ethics In Regards To Retargeting

Because it involves personal data and cookies, many marketers don't feel comfortable with the concept of retargeting. And if you truly feel that way, go right ahead and skip this step. *It's your business and you should run it how you see fit.* But you should know that without retargeting, you're missing out on a chance to seriously boost your sales. And as long as you are upfront with your customers about your data practice, such as with a popup agreement, you can rest assured that everything you're doing is perfectly legal and ethical.

The Basics Of Retargeting

Put simply, retargeting is the process of identifying customers who have shown interest in your product, then placing an ad for the aforementioned product in front of them again. The reason it works so well is simple – most people don't purchase something the first time they see it. Recent studies show that only 3% of first time visitors to a website will purchase an item *even if they already know they want it.*

But every additional time they see it, they become more and more likely to buy.

Here's how it works:

A customer visits your page, and clicks on a pair of blue shoes that they are interested in. Then, for whatever reason, they change their mind. They leave the page and forget all about it.

However, upon visiting your page, their browser was given what is known as a 'cookie.' A 'cookie' is the digital equivalent of a tracking device. It monitors what you do while visiting a specific page. That cookie then communicates the relevant information back to you – the marketer.

That cookie tells you that the customer was browsing blue shoes. The cookie can then be accessed to display ads for blue shoes

157

on third party sites or the visitor's social media page.

The customer logs into Instagram and sees the blue shoes again. The next week, they see the same shoes while browsing one of their favorite websites. And before you know it, they've decided – "You know what? I do want those shoes after all."

Customer surveys indicate that a majority of online shoppers don't mind cookies, because they only advertise relevant information. If that cookie can be used to advertise a sale or promotion, that's even better. And internet users always have the option of disabling or clearing their cookies at any time. This ensures that you are only marketing to people who want to be marketed to.

How To Set Up Your Tags On Google

Here comes the technical stuff. First, we are going to learn how to set up your retargeting campaign through Google Ads (you'll need an account, and this is a paid service). Then, we will discuss how to do the same thing through Facebook.

1. **Access/Create your Google Ads Account.**

2. **Select the tool icon, then select 'Audience Manager'**

3. **Select 'Audience Sources'**

4. **Under the heading 'Google Ads Tag,' select 'Set Up Tag.'**

5. **Select 'Collect data on specific actions people performed on your website to show personalized ads'**

6. **Select your business type.**

That's the first part! Super easy, if a little tedious. The following steps will require either a very basic knowledge of coding, or access to someone who does.

7. Select how you want to install the Google Ads tag.

For this step, you will be presented with three options.

If you select 'Install the tag yourself,' you will be given a short piece of code. Your job will be to embed the piece of code on the relevant areas of your page.

If you select 'email the tag to your webmaster,' you will be given the opportunity to send that tag to your tech person, who will know exactly what to do with it.

Now you've got the tag installed! Great, your second step is complete. You now have access to the behavior of anyone who visits your page. Lastly, we need to figure out what to do with that information. Let's keep moving!

8. Click Shared Library – › Audience Manager

9. Click The Blue Plus Sign – › Website Visitors

10. Select Your Desired Audience

You will have several options here. For example, you can target anyone who visited your page in the last 30, 60, or 90 days. You can also target visitors to a specific product page, which is how you can target exactly what they were looking for. One of the most effective methods is to target visitors to the checkout page. Those were the people who were closest to making a purchase, and they are the ones most likely to be persuaded by retargeting.

11. Select The Ads You Want Them To See

Here is the part where you choose what they see and how they see it. A banner bar is a particularly effective method, as it shows up at the top of a webpage they visit. But the only way to really know which ads perform best is - you guessed it - to split test.

How To Set Up Ads Using Facebook Pixel

This is the same concept, except instead of using Google, we will be using Facebook. Which will also allow you to retarget users on Instagram too. Much of this info is taken directly from Facebook's how to guide. I've done my best to simplify their text. Advanced social media users may get better results by going directly to the source.

(Note: A pixel is more or less the equivalent of a cookie.)

1. **Go To Facebook's Business Center and select 'Events Manager'**

2. **Click the green plus sign - › Connect Data Sources - › Web**

3. **Select 'Facebook Pixel' - › Connect**

4. **Name Your Pixel ie 'Recent Visitors'**

5. **Enter Your Page's URL**

Again, the first part is easy. Next, Facebook is going to give a line of code. It will then be our job to make sure that code is added to the website.

6. **Return To Events Manager**

7. **Click 'data sources'**

8. **Select the name of the pixel you just created**

9. **Select 'continue pixel set up'**

10. **Select 'Connect'**

11. **Select 'Install Code Manually'**

12. **Copy The Code**

13. **Install The Code (Or Have Someone Do It For You)**

Great! Now you have a direct line between your website and Facebook. The last step in this process is to use that information to begin showing ads on Facebook itself, and by extension, Instagram.

Here's how we do that:

1. **Return to your Ads Manager account**

2. **Select 'Events Manager'**

3. **Select 'Data Sources'**

4. **Select the relevant pixel**

5. **Select 'Settings'**

6. **Select 'Event Setup' – › 'Open Set Up Tool'**

7. **Enter Your Website**

8. **Select Event**

9. **Set Up parameters for that event**

This is the step where you will be able to select your audience and what ads they see.

10. 10- Select 'Finish Set Up'

Viola! You've done it. Now, you can begin to customize, and of course, test, your retargeting operation. If you are tech savvy enough to have completed everything in the previous section, you should have no trouble navigating this next part. But I remind you, if you find yourself stuck, don't hesitate to ask for help. We promise you, the results you get will make it well worth it.

What To Include In Your Retargeting Campaign

We've compiled the appropriate data and built a system that can be used to design your retargeting campaign. Now, the only question is: what should be included?

- The Product They Left In Their Shopping Cart

This should be your first, and most obvious choice. The customer has already shown enough interest to go all the way to the very last step of the process. Even if your checkout page is perfectly well designed (which it should be if you are in this step of the process), sometimes people just change their minds.

But it's unlikely that they went from complete interest to zero interest at all.

Maybe they took a look at their bank account and decided it was more responsible to make a purchase after they receive their next paycheck?

Maybe they wanted to check out a few of your competitors before making a final decision. That's not unreasonable. After all, there are so many options out there, a shopper should be expected to check them all out.

The reasons for a shopper leaving a product in a cart are essentially limitless.

The solution is simple.

Put that exact product in front of them somewhere else. Whether it is their Facebook feed or a website they browse on Google, go to where they hang out and remind them that you exist.

Maybe that customer got a bonus at work. Now they are ready to spend some extra cash. Good thing your ad was there to remind them about that product they were interested in.

Maybe your customer checked out the competition and found them too similar to make a decision. A well placed ad might just be the ticket you need to tip the

scales in your favor.

If you understand the process, it is relatively easy to retarget customers who left items in their shopping carts. Just add a cookie to your checkout page and use it to identify the item in question.

– Items Similar To Previous Purchases

If you've already made some sales, this is a great way to get that customer coming back over and over again. You can program your retargeting ad to market similar items to people who have already shown that they like your product.

Research shows that customers are anywhere from 60- 75% more likely to click on a targeted ad than a cold ad (which is a generic advertisement meant for anybody). So take advantage of this statistic. You've found your ideal customer, now it is time to make the most of the relationship.

163

- Items That Enhance a Previous Purchase

This is great for businesses that sell memberships, subscriptions, educational content, etc. For example, if you have successfully hosted an 'Intro To Real Estate' webinar, you could retarget those people with an ad selling a class called 'Intermediate Real Estate.' And so on and so forth. The possibilities are endless.

Depending on what you produce, you have many different options regarding how you approach this part of the process. Make sure that you are tailoring this to your business's strengths. When in doubt, do a little testing.

- How Retargeting Can Actually Get You New Leads

At its core, retargeting is meant to turn potential customers into paying customers. But, if done correctly, it can actually be so much more.

In a way, retargeting is simply a form of data gathering. And as we all know, data is everything when it comes to CRO.

The data you use to create your retargeting campaign can be used to create what we refer to as 'lookalike audiences.'

Lookalike audiences are made up of customers that you have yet to make contact with, but who share key characteristics of your existing customers.

You can manage this information manually if you'd like.

For example, you see that 85% of the people you are retargeting are middle aged people in the midwest.

Now you know where to direct your advertising budget.

You can also employ the massive databases afforded to you Facebook and Google. Their advanced metrics can narrow down your targets to people who behave the same way online as your existing customers.

They visit the same websites, read the same blogs, and have the same purchasing habits.

This is where 'good' turns into 'great.'

You are now simultaneously converting existing leads and creating new ones. Now we're talking about real, exponential growth.

The Science Behind Retargeting

You can think of retargeting the same way you would think about making a new friend.

Would you ever walk up to a total stranger and ask them if they would help you move into a new house? Or maybe if they could pick you up at the airport this weekend?

Of course not! They'd say no and try to get away from you as fast as possible.

But ask a friend, and hopefully, they'll be willing to help you out.

Here's why: As friends, you value each other. You've taken the time to get to know one another. You communicate regularly, you respect each other, and you trust each other.

Getting a person to buy your product or sign up for your course reflects the same process.

Sometimes, when I'm watching YouTube, I'll see an ad for somebody claiming to be some sort of sales guru. They'll make big promises about how they can turn me into a millionaire so that I can travel the world on a helicopter drinking champagne. Then, just out of curiosity, I Google them. What do I always find?

Nothing.

Maybe they have a website making the same outlandish promises and begging me to sign up for their course.

But that's it.

There's no useful free material, no thoughtful blog posts, no insights into the opportunity that their service will provide.

Why on earth would I consider giving them my hard earned money?

It is essential that you provide something of value before you expect them to hand over their money. Your retargeting campaign is a great opportunity to do this. You can advertise your newest video lesson or share a testimonial from a recent customer. In time, you'll start to build the foundations of a real relationship.

Familiarity

Wendy's Founder and fast food icon Dave Thomas is famous for observing that many people are willing to forego excitement for the comfort of familiarity.

He built hundreds of restaurants across the country, all with the exact same design and the exact same menu.

He knew that most people wouldn't stop for a burger the first time they saw one of his franchises. Maybe not even the second or third time.

166

But sooner or later, after seeing the exact same restaurant over and over again, many people would feel ready to try it. Some of them even became lifelong customers, knowing that they could be in any city in America and still get their favorite burger.

Today, there are nearly seven thousand Wendy's Restaurants in the United States alone.

The success of Dave Thomas's strategy speaks to the importance of building familiarity with your customers. They need to know that you're consistent - that you are going to provide them with high quality service every time.

Retargeting campaigns are the perfect way of building familiarity. Customers may not click the first, second, or third time. But eventually, with enough hard work and data driven analysis, the clicks will start to come. And with clicks, comes conversions.

Conclusion

Retargeting is an essential part of any online sales operation. Because of its highly technical nature, many marketers shy away from it. Don't be one of them. Take the time to master these techniques or hire a pro.

As you optimize your retargeting campaign, ask yourself the following questions:

☐ Am I retargeting the right people?

☐ Am I getting the most out of Google and Facebook's features?

☐ Am I retargeting the correct products or services?

☐ Am I offering something of value?

☐ Am I building familiarity with customers?

☐ Have I run enough tests to know that my retargeting campaign is fully optimized?

Chapter Fourteen:

Beyond 10X With Sales Psychology

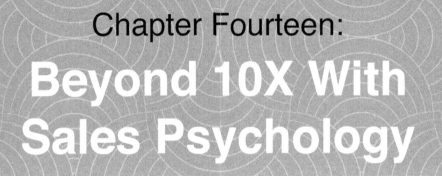

"Whether you think you can or whether you think you can't,
you're right!"
– Henry Ford

In this chapter, you will learn:

- ✓ How To Build The Confidence You Need To Start Making Sales

- ✓ How To Eliminate The Fear Of Failure

- ✓ The True Nature Of How Customers Make Decisions

- ✓ How To Boost Sales By Presenting Opportunities

- ✓ How To Stay Motivated In Your Pursuit Of CRO Mastery

If you've made it this far, let me be the first to say: *congratulations*.

Whether you started this book as a total beginner or an experienced marketer, I am confident that you have encountered many concepts that will inevitably improve your operation's CRO performance.

This next section is written specifically for those who have mastered, or at least dramatically improved in, every skill we have discussed so far.

If you skipped ahead, I urge you to go back and slowly make your way through the fundamental skill set that makes eCommerce so lucrative. Come back later, and I assure you, the following information will be so much more valuable to you.

We've talked a lot about statistics - about the large percentage of shops that never make a single sale, and how improving your CRO by a mere 2% might be enough to keep your shop alive. In this section, we're going to leave statistics behind.

We're going to talk in more vague terms, such as "the few" and "the many." We're going to look at ideas that can't always be measured.

We're going to talk in depth about the timeless principles of salesmanship.

Our goal is not only to study the psychology and sales language of the buyer, but the psychology of the seller.

That's you.

Take a step back from your work and think of why you're actually doing this.

You could have taken a safer career path – one with a guaranteed salary and consistent, if unfulfilling, work.

From my experience, however, people who get involved in eCommerce, especially those that are starting their own operation, are cut from a different cloth.

There is an unfortunate myth pervading the world of eCommerce, which is that it is easy.

This idea is often aggressively marketed, as well intentioned, by naive young marketers. They start a project, build a Shopify store, then get overwhelmed at all the steps they hadn't considered. And again, they tend to abandon the project, and with it, their dreams of controlling their financial destiny.

I can't stand hearing these stories.
I hear them all the time, and they never cease to bother me. And that's why I wrote this book.

As I've said before, I was lucky enough to be working in this industry since long before it became such a powerful cultural force. By happenstance, I was there to watch the techniques get developed, to see the wheat separated from the chaff.

Sure, I went to great lengths to master my craft and sought out the best advice a businessperson could possibly receive, but so much of my success was the result of being in the right place at the right time.

That time, however, is gone forever.

Now, if someone wants to learn how to make sales online, they probably start with a google search.

They are quickly inundated with an overwhelming amount of material.
With no clear place to start, it is almost impossible for them not to get overwhelmed. Not to mention the fact that much of the information they find is trivial at best and fraudulent at worst.

It is an awfully difficult way to learn anything at all, much less a skill as complex as CRO.

So I thought to myself, what if I compiled all my knowledge in one, well organized, easily actionable Book. After all, I've achieved success I never dreamed of.

Why not share my good fortune with the countless hard workers out there who just need a little guidance?

Sharing this information is meant to let you directly into my mind - my motivations, my goals, my aspirations. The psychology behind "me."

In the following section, we are going to discuss the psychology behind "you."

Every individual is different, and I'm certainly not asking you to conform to any rigid mindset. But I can absolutely help you identify what thought patterns may be holding you back.

And I can show you how to replace them with more beneficial thought patterns. I can show you how the greatest salesman trained themselves to think.

Hopefully, you will be able to utilize these concepts to achieve the kind of success that I have been lucky enough to achieve.

How To Build Successful Sales Confidence

Maybe you have heard of the popular phrase "Fake it until you make it." Frankly, I don't find this advice to be all that helpful. I believe it is much better to sit down and truly educate yourself before you present yourself as an expert. (Which is why I've advised you not to read this section until you have a firm understanding of the specifics of CRO.)

Confidence comes with practice, failure, success, more failure, and then more success.

You need to learn to separate yourself from the results of your actions.

If a client is rude to you and chooses not to do business with you, don't take it personally. It doesn't mean you're a bad salesperson. It more likely means that your pitch was too soft or too aggressive, or the value was not understood. Or maybe that person just didn't need what you were selling.

The key thing is to not take it to heart.

 Just consider every missed sales opportunity to be a data point you can use to improve.

A more useful quote would be this one, attributed to Thomas Edison:

"I have not failed, I have just found 10,000 ways that do not work."

These words, coming from a man whose innovations have shaped modern society, should be a source of great comfort to anyone who has struggled to succeed in any business pursuit.

Did you pour endless hours into your online business, only to find out that your friends or siblings were your only customer?

That's okay. That's good in fact. Every successful marketer I know was once in the same boat.

Did you try redesigning the site, or maybe even starting an entirely new operation, only to see the same results? (maybe this time you made a sale to both your mother and your father)

Even better. Now you're way ahead of the game.

By the time you start work on your third, fourth, and fifth projects, you will have already accumulated more knowledge than most. Combine that with the specific techniques in this book, and I can almost guarantee that you will start to see results.

The problem is that we are so easily discouraged. It is only natural to want to give up after consecutive failures. The key is to persevere, not take any loss personally, and refuse to give up until you are where you want to be. You got this!

Moving Past Your Fears And Limitations

Fear is a powerful thing. And in the right context, fear can be a good thing. I'm afraid of getting hit by a car, so I look both ways before I cross a busy road.

But all too often, fear manifests itself in ways that don't benefit us at all. Let's take a look at some of the most common sales fears, and how to overcome them.

- "I'm afraid of looking foolish."

Yeah, I'll admit, some of my friends looked at me funny all those years ago when I said I was going to make a living in online business. Nowadays, those same friends come to me for advice on how to make more money. And I'm happy to share!

The truth is, people will always question you for going against the grain. Pick any major figure who has helped to lead the technological revolution, and I can assure you, people told them they were nuts. Whether it is a global figure like Barbara Corcoran or Jeff Bezos, or the woman down the street from you who makes a living selling handmade jewelry, I promise you, somewhere along the way, someone thought they were crazy.

It's way too easy to give cliche advice such as "Don't care what other people think."

In fact, you should care what people think.

You should care what they'll think when they see you start to live out your dreams.

You should care what they think when they view you as an inspiration.

You should care what they think when they enjoy spending time with you, because you have become so successful and generous with your wisdom.

- "I'm afraid that I don't have the skills I need to succeed."

Maybe you don't! But skills can be learned. That's why we've broken this book down into small digestible chapters.

If I tell you to "become a master of CRO," of course you'll be intimidated, and possibly think that you can't do it.

But what if I tell you to "Study these specific concepts for the next couple of weeks and learn how to design an effective product grid?" Suddenly, it's not so scary.

Break your goals down into small, manageable steps. Even if you only make tiny amounts of progress at first, your efforts will start to snowball eventually.

Trying to get in shape? Do one pushup. The next day, try two. So on and so forth.

The exact same principle can be applied to CRO.

Spend a week just looking at landing pages. See which ones you like and which ones you don't. Then, the following week, get yourself an account at ClickFunnels or Wordpress and try to design something yourself.

Don't expect anything close to perfection.

Just create something.

From there, identify what you can do to make this more closely resemble the landing pages that impressed you.

Do you need better graphics but you don't know how to design them? Hire a freelancer on Fiverr or Upwork.

Struggling with the copy? Just try to write one good sentence. Maybe consider sharing that sentence on a Facebook group, where a host of professional copywriters are always willing to share their advice.

Whatever you do, remember that action is the cure to fear. If you're busy putting in the work, your mind will become so consumed that it won't have any room left for fears and worries.

All it takes is getting started.

How Your Customer Thinks

Earlier in the book, we mentioned that sales has always been an integral part of human society. No human being can survive entirely on their own - at some point, they're gonna need goods and services that they can't provide for themselves.

We start making sales decisions from the earliest days of our young adulthood - when we're out of the house and suddenly, we need to decide what food to buy.

But our sales history goes even further back than that. As young kids, we saw advertisements on television for all the exciting things we wanted - a trip to Disney World, the newest Playstation game, a happy meal. The desire to buy, sell, trade, give, and take is an essential part of our upbringing.

This brings me to my first, and most valuable point regarding your customer's psychological make up:

People Want To Buy

How many people do you know that are 100% satisfied with every single aspect of their life?

People who are in perfect health, have no wants or desires, are not interested in any sort of new experiences? My guess is zero. If you do encounter this person, don't waste your time on them. That is the only type of person who can't be marketed towards.

For every other person on earth, I guarantee, there is something they want. Or something they need. And if presented in the right way, they'll be happy to pay whatever you're asking.

Perhaps you are familiar with the stereotype of the sleazy used-car salesman - always using high pressure sales tactics, trying to sell unnecessary add-ons, making promises they can't follow through with. Stereotypes like this often dissuade people from getting involved in sales.

When the truth is, a good salesperson is genuinely out to help their clients, while using a healthy blend of sales language. They have no interest in taking advantage of someone. They want to build long lasting, meaningful relationships.

The online equivalent of the sleazy salesman might be a website loaded with aggressive pop- up ads, hidden links, and blatantly untrue information. When you mention online marketing to someone, this might be the unfortunate image that comes into their minds.

Those ineffective and dishonest techniques betray a simple truth.

People have more disposable income than ever before. For many, shopping is a hobby. You don't need to be aggressive, they're going to come to you. They want nothing more than the thrill they get when your product arrives on their front porch.

So keep that in mind as you design your page. People want to be there.

Make them feel welcome.

Make it easy for them to stay.

Make it easy for them to shop, and make it easy for them to check out.

Gains And Losses

In his book "The Psychology of Sales", famous salesman Brian Tracy wrote that people's primary reason for making a purchase is usually either a desire for gain or a fear of loss. If they aren't gaining something valuable or losing something burdensome, they probably won't be willing to spend a dime. Identify what your service is helping people gain or lose. Common things include:

- Gains

- Wealth
- Knowledge
- Pleasure
- Experience
- Health
- Fun
- Self Expression
- Enlightenment

- Losses

- Illness
- Debt
- Boredom
- Discomfort
- Ignorance

Think of the last three big purchases you made. Identify what you gained or lost by buying that product.

The more things you can list, the more I'm willing to bet you spent on those products.

Emphasize these points as effectively as you can in your copy.

New Opportunities

These days, buying the same old products, systems, or solutions, feels like groundhog day for the average consumer. Besides selling the typical things that offer something to be fixed or renovated, providing them a replacement or new opportunity is a far more exciting way that will attract many more valuable customers.

To further build off this important idea, let's think of the people whose innovations have truly altered the world. When Steve Jobs presented the iPhone, it wasn't just a cool new gadget. It was the beginning of a new era. Life has become more exciting and more convenient since this invention. That's because Jobs wasn't selling a product. He was selling an opportunity.

Think of what Elon Musk is offering with Tesla. It's not just a fast car. People already have fast cars. It's not even a status symbol. People can show off their wealth in any number of ways.

But, why do you and I frequently gravitate to these examples of success?

Because you are an entrepreneur.

Someone who is willing to embrace a new era. While the rest of the population talks endlessly about how bad things are, you are looking boldly into the future.

That is what I mean when I tell you to sell opportunities.

Coming up with the next greatest opportunity may seem like far more work, but the payoff is exponentially greater. In fact, the great Dan Kennedy once said "If you will STOP SELLING STUFF! – and start selling OPPORTUNITY, you'll see a marked difference in the response. This is, in fact, the greatest opportunity to transform advertising or marketing results!"

When a product is presented as an opportunity it just feels fresh, new, and is welcomed with much less resistance. The keyword "Opportunity" is even in the main headline of the book cover – so it must be effective, right?

Spending a good amount of time to really think about what product or service you can work on crafting for your customers is definitely a highly valuable and recommended exercise!

What Keeps Your Clients Up At Night?

As we stated before, very few people are 100% satisfied with their lives. That's just human nature. Everyone wants more. People are always wondering what else is out there. It is often a vague feeling, one that is difficult to articulate.

Your job as a salesman is to identify exactly what your client feels is missing. Then, you show them that you have what they want.

Get them excited about it. After that, they will be happy to give you their attention, and more importantly, their business.

So think about this ever important question - what keeps your clients up at night?

Here are a few of the most common things that I have encountered from my years of talking with countless customers from every walk of life.

- Ambition

This is a big one. Certain people are wired to always want more. They want power, status, and money. And that is a good thing! There is no substitute for the feeling of self worth that comes with a position of power. Can you help your clients bring their ambitions to life? If you can, you are going to be a very successful businessperson.

Try not to focus on small issues.

Small issues can be solved on their own.

Hearing about solutions to small problems doesn't excite people.

Think of major problems, do the necessary work to find meaningful solutions, and then confidently tell your clients what you can do for them.

- Fear

Even the most successful people on earth have probably spent some sleepless nights worrying about the future.

Again, this is a part of the human condition.

People are afraid of running out of money, not being able to take care of their families, or not fulfilling their potential.

I've heard these sentiments from so many people, and that is a big part of why I wanted to write this book. While the material is very technical and in-depth, at its core, this is a book about getting what you want.

Whether it is CRO, or whatever opportunity you are presenting, if you are able to help people overcome their fears, you are going to be very successful with sales.

- Boredom

So many people have untapped potential. And while this is inherently a good thing, it can be awfully uncomfortable to sit with.

If you were capable of running a successful eCommerce operation but instead, you were stuck working an unfulfilling minimum wage job, it is easy to imagine that you would have quite a few sleepless nights.

This book focuses on a specific niche - people who want to make more sales online. Think of your ideal client. What do they wish they were doing? What would give them the thrill they need to feel alive and bring their dreams to fruition?
Be specific!

In this book, for example, I didn't just show you how to start an eCommerce store. Anyone can do that. I got into the nitty gritty, the stuff that most people never take the time to understand. And you know what? I would bet my readers were happy to spend their time digging in! Because it is a passion for them. People want to embrace their passions. You show them how to do it, and they will become a customer for life.

What Are Your Clients Top Three Daily Frustrations?

Let's go back to the example of Steve Jobs and the iPhone. It is safe to say that this is one of the most earth shattering inventions of all time. But let's look at it from a smaller perspective. What simple, daily frustrations were eliminated because of the iPhone?

Do you remember a time when you had to memorize or write down the phone number of every person you know?

Or a time when you had to spend ages looking through a giant phonebook to find the number of a local business?

It's hard to imagine now, but within many of our lifetimes, that was a daily reality. How frustrating! Now, every number is in your pocket at all times. You can get in touch with just about anyone *instantly*.

Have you ever tried to read a map of a city you've never been to? One of those big, foldable maps that looks like it came out of a movie? Imagine using one of those to plan a road trip nowadays. It would drive you crazy! But thanks to Steve's invention, nowadays, you can get detailed directions to just about any location on earth.

For the music lovers out there, think of your old CD collection. Remember how easily they got scratched up and needed to be replaced? And remember how difficult it was to try and change

CDs while you were driving? Maybe you almost drove off the road! Nowadays, every song you can imagine can be accessed on your iPhone at all times.

You can even control your music with your voice. Yet another daily frustration that has become a thing of the past.

Now chances are, you are not going to invent the next iPhone.

Developments like that come around once a generation. But don't let that stop you from aiming big.

There must be one simple problem that you have a solution for. What little inconvenience can you get rid of with your service or product?

 Think long and hard about this, because it can really put you in the mindset you need to be in to find success.

Follow the Trends

The business world is always evolving.

Over the past few years, progress has taken place at such a breakneck speed that it is almost impossible to keep up. And every changing trend should be viewed as an opportunity. People are hungry for new technologies, new ways of thinking, and better ways of getting things done.

If you can improve someone's work/life balance, that's even better. Carefully observe the trends you're seeing in the business world.

Look for your opening, you may be surprised at what you are capable of.

Who Else Is Selling Something Similar?

Success is not a zero sum game.

Just because someone else is doing well at one thing, that doesn't mean you can't jump in yourself. Think Coke and Pepsi.

You should carefully observe the people who are succeeding in a field that you are interested in.

Ambitious people are often very open to sharing their experiences with like minded individuals. And you never know where your fellow entrepreneurs are going to end up. Build strong relationships, be honest and open, and learn from the people around you.

The Decision Making Process

Certain people are 'pre-programed' to act in certain ways. People who work in science are naturally extremely analytical. Parents are always thinking of ways to improve their children's lives. Try to put yourself in your clients' shoes. Think of how they make their decisions. Make it easy for them to choose you as the person who will fix their problems.

Conclusion

I could write an entire book all about my fascination with sales. It's amazing to learn this language and how, with enough practice, you can see great profits from your labor.

As you continue on your journey, you will meet many entrepreneurs, all with varying levels of success. But the ones with the most fulfilling lives will always be the ones who understand these sales principles in addition to the intricacies of their chosen profession.

In conclusion to this final chapter, here are a few questions you can ask yourself:

☐ What's stopping me from getting started?

☐ Am I willing to put myself out there to achieve my dreams and goals?

☐ Have I truly deepened my understanding of how customers think?

☐ What opportunities can I offer my customers?

☐ How can I solve my customers' most pressing problems?

☐ Am I committed to continuing to grow and learn?

☐ How can I continue pursuing my goal of CRO mastery?

Conclusion:

To CRO Infinity And Beyond!

What To Do Next

A big congratulations on making it to the end. I sincerely want to thank you for joining me on this journey. I hope that this book was as enjoyable for you to read as it was for me to write. It is my genuine hope that I have provided you with tremendous value on exactly how to grow your conversions by 10x and more!

I encourage you to revisit any topics that are of specific interest to you. Here is a quick recap of what we have covered:

1. I shared the story of how I became a CRO expert. I explained that I did it through non-stop trial and error. I also had the privilege of learning from some of the finest business minds in the world.

2. We explored the basic concepts of CRO. We showed you how to calculate your own CRO and we explained how your profits could skyrocket if you were to improve.

3. In the middle of the book we explored every step of your sales funnel. We talked about designing the perfect customer experience - from the landing page to the instant they checkout.

4. We discussed how to create meaningful relationships with your customers by providing real, tangible value to their lives. We also took an in-depth look at how to communicate with them through social media, blogging, and email. We emphasized the importance of building two-way relationships - not just talking to your customers but listening to what they have to say.

5. We discussed specific data analysis strategies that can be used to optimize your UX. We emphasized the importance of testing as many elements of our operation as possible.

6. We explored the psychology of sales. We discussed how

to get yourself into the mindset for success so that you can start achieving your goals. And we discussed the importance of offering customers opportunities.

Now, there is only one thing left for you to do:

Get to growing those conversions!

Need a little extra boost to get your conversions to skyrocket faster, and become more profitable than ever before? Please feel free to schedule a call with our team. We'd love to hear how we can help you!

CROProfits.com/Call

Success is not something that only happens to a select few. It is there for everyone. It is there for you. You have greatness within you to offer the world. Now get out there and do it!

Sincerely,

Anthony La Rocca
Founder and CEO @ CRO Profits

— - - - - - - - - -

BONUS AREA

Included free with your copy of this book, I have added an **exclusive bonus area** to help you get even more conversions!

130 Billion Dollar Funnel Breakdown

- One of the favorite funnels that my coaching clients love me to break down is,
  Home Depot USA. This is one of the largest B2B online stores, which generates over 130 Billion USD per year! I pull back the curtains and show you all areas of this behemoth and how you can utilize their best practices to boost your business profits, all while using Grow 10X With CRO to bring it all together!

  - Visit CROProfits.com/BillionFunnel

The Heatmap Success Blueprint

- Let's get you selling! In this video training, I will walk you through, step-by-step, the true power of using heatmap software such as Hotjar. Learning to use tools like this can allow for a dramatic sales increase in as little as 14 days!

  - Visit CROProfits.com/TripleSales

3 Step CRO Playbook

- We are very excited to be sharing the best split tests to perform to see rapid boosts to your conversions and sales giving every business owner, entrepreneur, service provider a consistent split testing routine to follow for success.

  This playbook will give you the most important parts of pushing a sale over the edge to help you maximize those conversions!

  - Visit CROProfits.com/3StepPlaybook

The CRO Hotlist

- In this bonus module you will learn the Top 5 best websites that every business owner, entrepreneur, service providing business must study to obtain ultimate conversion domination to Grow 10X and beyond!

  It is very difficult to obtain any sort of growth with conversions without constantly studying the best-of-the-best, and so in this hotlist we are going to teach you just that!

  - Visit CROProfits.com/TheCROHotList

Top 20 Ultimate Tools

– As you know, conversion optimization is critical for the success of any business. If you are unable to convert your visitors into customers, your traffic becomes worthless.

You will now get access to our ultimate top 20 picks for CRO tools we have used and have proven to be the most effective tools on a small budget.

– Visit CROProfits.com/Top20Tools

About the Author

Anthony La Rocca is the founder and CEO of CRO Profits, a conversion growth agency that has launched revenues upwards of 1000% for some of the world's most recognized brands.

Anthony is a 14 time best selling course creator (WarriorForum.com) and has coached hundreds of students all over the world, teaching them how to successfully boost the effectiveness of their online business and funnels. Anthony has earned a reputation for his ability to easily break down any challenging business goals, and turn them into a positive ROI.

All inquiries for podcast appearances, video interviews, and speaking gigs can be sent to marketing@CROProfits.com

Printed in Great Britain
by Amazon